D0265791

THE OCTAVE OF THE NATIVITY

*Essays and notes on ten
liturgical reconstructions
for Christmas*

Edited by

Nick Sandon

BRITISH BROADCASTING CORPORATION

Published by
BBC Books
A division of BBC Enterprises Ltd
Woodlands, 80 Wood Lane, London W12 0TT

First published 1984
Reissued 1987
ISBN 0 563 20325 0

© BRITISH BROADCASTING CORPORATION 1984

Printed in Great Britain by Belmont Press, Northampton

Contents

Illustrations

Acknowledgements

For permission to reproduce copyright illustrations the following are gratefully acknowledged: Architectural Press Ltd (page 48). BBC Hulton Picture Library (54). The Curators of the Bodleian Library (37, 62). The British Library (44, 71, 72). The British Museum (52). Biblioteca Apostolica Vaticana (66). Bibliothèque Municipale, Laon (40). Alban Caroe (59).

Introduction

For most people in the West today, liturgy must be a remote and irrelevant concept. We live in a far more secular world than our ancestors, and in our worship (as in all aspects of our life) we put a much lower value than they did on formality, discipline, dignity and convention. We find a sense of mateyness more comfortable than a sense of awe. To a medieval or Renaissance man, however, a sense of the religious and the habit of formal worship were inescapable aspects of being alive. Public worship was a meticulously ordered series of words and actions whose unchanging nature stabilised an unpredictable world, and whose very complexity (so often criticised by 'reformers') put man's creative capacity to the best possible use in the praise of his Creator.

In the Middle Ages and the Renaissance, liturgy and art in all its forms were intimately associated; the latter was used to adorn the former, but was also influenced by it. The stereotyped action and literary formulae of medieval romances have a strongly liturgical element, and the story of the Sangrail in the Arthurian cycle is permeated by resonances from the Mass. Several poets even parodied the items of the Mass in a secular context, as in the 'Mass of the Gamblers' in the *Carmina Burana* manuscript. The style of plainsong was often affected by liturgical requirements: a chant accompanying an action, such as the Introit, would tend to have a somewhat utilitarian character in order not to distract the attention of the participants, whereas a chant associated with a scriptural reading, such as the Gradual, would be as characterful and beautiful as possible in order to elevate the listeners' minds to a state of maximum receptivity. In polyphonic church music, too, the style and form of a composition could be influenced by liturgical considerations: in most polyphonic Credo settings there is a full cadence and pause after 'descendit de caelis', because at this point the choir knelt or turned to the altar. The liturgical division of a text between solo singers and the choir was often reflected by leaving the words of one of the groups in plainsong when setting the item in polyphony.

The magnificent quire screens of medieval churches were not merely decorative; they supported lofts from which the Epistle and Gospel were sung on important days. Doorways in churches (and even archways in external buttresses) were positioned to permit the processions called for by the liturgy. Liturgical motifs (particularly the moment of Elevation) dominated the illuminations in late medieval service books. Some liturgical expressions and concepts have survived into modern life. The 'first form' and 'second form' of our schooldays are named after the junior and intermediate stalls of the medieval choir, while to be 'installed' meant to take one's seat in the choirstalls (usually for the first time, with some ceremony). When we speak of something being 'of a higher grade' than another, we are harking back to the different steps (Latin *gradus*) that the choirstalls were on, and perhaps also to the steps ascending to the altar that were allocated respectively to the subdeacon, deacon and priest. Our 'red-letter days' derive from the use of red ink to denote special days in medieval liturgical calendars. Our 'anthem' comes from the 'antiphon' (Latin *antiphona*) of early Christian times.

As a musicologist, my interest in liturgy arose out of problems which I encountered in medieval and Renaissance music, fundamentally from the question that all musicologists should try to answer: 'Why is this music like it is?' A high proportion of the music that survives from the Middle Ages and Renaissance was written for use in church, practically always in some liturgical context. A knowledge of liturgy can often help us to determine the intended context of particular compositions, like many of the so-called 'motets' of Josquin, and even their places of origin. We will also be better equipped to suggest explanations for peculiar features in certain compositions: for example, some of the Credo settings in the Old Hall manuscript begin at 'Factorem' rather than the usual 'Patrem'. Could this indicate provenance from a Benedictine foundation such as St Mary's Abbey, York, where after the celebrant's intonation the rulers sang 'Patrem omnipotentem', and the choir came in only at 'Factorem'? A little elementary liturgical knowledge would spare editors the embarrassment of supplying Gloria and Credo intonations which simply did not exist at the time or in the locality of the setting in question, or of publishing an *alternatim* Magnificat without the plainchant for the intervening verses.

I believe that a liturgical reconstruction is not merely an academic exercise (albeit a productive one); it is also the most artistically effective and instructive way of presenting medieval and Renaissance church music. Most of this repertory was meant for no other context than that of a religious devotion, and it works much less well in any other kind of environment. To present the five movements of a Dufay or Palestrina Mass as five consecutive items in a concert makes them sound monotonous; to intersperse them with secular material creates incongruity. The obvious answer is to present them in association with the material that the composer envisaged: the chant (or arrangements of it) and the spoken texts of the service itself. When one hears such music performed in this way one becomes conscious for the first time of a whole world of local contrast, internal relationship and overall planning that one could never have imagined. Whether or not the reconstruction is planned as a religious celebration, and whether or not we ourselves are believers, every constituent takes on an enhanced stature, because it plays an organic role in an imposing structure. Until now, one of the most depressing aspects of the early-music revival has been its obsession with the trivial; it may be that the liturgical reconstruction represents the most effective means by which we can come to an understanding of what medieval and Renaissance composers considered to be truly important.

The 'science' of liturgical reconstruction (if that is not too pretentious a term) is a relatively new one. It has not been a preoccupation with liturgiologists, although it is naturally implicit in much of the work that they do. Reconstruction has its obvious problems: sources of information for particular places and periods (such as late medieval Canterbury) may not survive; chant readings may be corrupt. Some difficulties, however, are less predictable. Of these, perhaps the most important and frustrating is the failure of so many sources to provide instructions and material for the most mundane aspects of the service: to give a tone for the prayers or the 'Dominus vobiscum', for example, or to set out precisely the processional route on a particular day. Such things were omitted because they were part of a continuing tradition; they were so well known that there was simply no point in writing them down. In such cases we have to utilise the information in comparable sources, or simply make a more-or-less informed guess as to what was done. Other areas of present uncertainty include performance style in plainchant, the size of polyphonic choirs and the ways in which they sang, and the use of the organ. Copious information on these and other topics waits to be sifted and appraised (which is not to belittle the work already being done).

These ten reconstructions are an early step along a lengthy road. They are indebted to previous work, in particular to Bruno Turner's recreation of the *Missa in Gallicantu* broadcast by BBC Radio 3 in the early 1970s. We have deliberately imposed limitations, leaving unexplored the Eastern liturgies and restricting ourselves largely to Mass. I must thank my coeditors and contributors to this booklet for the commitment which they have given to a daunting enterprise; in particular I acknowledge their contribution to the introductory notes printed elsewhere in these pages. I wish also to record my gratitude to Hugh Keyte, who conceived the project and saw it through its early stages, and to Clive Wearing, who steered it to completion.

Nick Sandon
University of Exeter
On the feast of the Purification of Our Lady, 1984

This booklet has been revised for the second transmission of the reconstructions at Christmas 1987. The first broadcast of the series in 1984 stimulated an unprecedented response; more than a thousand listeners wrote to express their appreciation, while fewer than ten communicated negative reactions. The intervening three years have seen an enhanced interest in performing early church music liturgically, and a corresponding growth of expertise in doing so. In consequence the mistakes in these reconstructions may now be more obvious, but I hope that listeners may nevertheless enjoy the opportunity to hear them again.

Nick Sandon
University College, Cork
On the feast of St Michael the Archangel, 1987

The Idea and Purpose of Liturgy

The Reverend Michael J. Moreton

Liturgy is as old as the Church. It was never introduced or added to the life of the Church, but was the setting in which the Church attained self-consciousness and eventually autonomy. When the first Evangelist, Mark, wrote of Jesus entering the synagogue, he was probably referring to a practice with which the earliest disciples were themselves familiar and which they still continued. With Mark's reviser Matthew, however, the case may be different; for he introduces a refinement, saying that Jesus entered into *their* synagogue, which suggests that Christians had in his time withdrawn from the synagoges now dominated by the Pharisees, and formed synagogues of their own.

What Christians had to say about Jesus, his significance for Israel and eventually for the Gentiles, was to a very large extent founded upon the scriptures, that is to say, upon the Old Testament. The scripture rolls were kept in the synagogue, and it was in the synagogue that they were read and expounded. The units of which the Gospels are composed were profoundly influenced by the scriptures in regard to both their form and content.

Given the intimate relationship that exists between the New Testament and the Old, therefore, it is no surprise to discover that the liturgy of the synagogue has deeply influenced the liturgy of the Church. The basic structure of the synagogue liturgy – lessons, sermon, prayers – has determined the basic structure of the first part of the Christian liturgy, known to Orthodox as 'the liturgy of the catechumens' (those under instruction), or under a modern title as 'the liturgy of the Word'. It is also arguable that the first part of the Greek eucharistic prayer – the opening dialogue, act of praise and Sanctus – derives from the liturgy of the Greek-speaking synagogue.

But it was not only the liturgy of the synagogue which was in part transmitted to the liturgy of the Church as the starting-point of its development. There was also the para-liturgy of the Jewish home. The weekly Sabbath was a peculiarly Jewish institution, with nothing corresponding to it in the Greek or Roman world. It was inaugurated by a meal for the whole household, which was an occasion of rejoicing. The head of the household took a cup of wine and pronounced over it a blessing addressed to God in thanksgiving for his gift, coupled with the blessing of the day, and similarly with the bread. It was this weekly Sabbath meal which underlay the weekly eucharist of the Church, although from a very early date the eucharist was transferred from the Sabbath to the first day of the week.

Again, the Jewish calendar also left its mark on the development of the Christian liturgy. Two festivals in particular profoundly influenced the character of the eucharist: the Passover, by virtue of its association with the institution of the eucharist, and the Day of Atonement, which has deeply coloured its meaning. Thus liturgy is the setting of the life of the Church from the time of Christ, and is inseparable from the Church's understanding of itself, its message and its mission.

THE CHRISTIAN LITURGY AND THE CHRISTIAN GOSPEL

At no point, then, is Christian liturgy annexed to the Christian gospel. But the Christian liturgy, founded upon the liturgy of the synagogue, derives its essential character from the Christian gospel. Now the gospel has as its root the resurrection of Christ. The written Gospels – and this is an insight elaborated if not gained in the first place by modern critical scholarship – were 'written backwards'; for their underlying presupposition is the resurrection of Christ. It is this datum which transforms the liturgy inherited by the Church from the synagogue.

The Gospel traditions of the manifestations of the risen Lord involve corporate experience more often than individual experience, and indeed individual experience is rather the exception. The corporate experience is said to inspire in those who see Him 'worship'. Thus the reverence that is reserved for God is transferred to the risen Christ. The most far-reaching confession of faith found in the Gospels is attributed to doubting Thomas, namely, 'My Lord and my God'. Moreover, in a number of instances the appearance of the risen Christ is placed in the setting of a meal: on the road to Emmaus and in Jerusalem (Luke), on the shore of the sea of Tiberias (John), and in the long supplement to the earliest Gospel (Mark). This fact can hardly be without significance in the Church, when the eucharist was in origin associated with a meal. Furthermore, the appearances of the risen Lord are accompanied by the signs of His passion. The wounds of His crucifixion are 'shown' and 'seen'.

While the future general resurrection of the dead was and remains part of the faith of Israel, it is the distinctive mark of the Christian gospel that Christ has already risen from the dead – summed up in a single Greek word at the tomb, *ēgerthē* ('He is risen'). For Christ, in taking the bread and then the cup into His hands, foreshadowed His death, and invested it with sacrificial meaning. Developing from this tradition, the eucharist has accordingly always been understood as a sacrificial rite in which, as St Paul says, the death of the Lord is proclaimed.

Liturgical development from the synagogue to the Church may be summed up in this way. The death and resurrection of Christ impelled the Church to adopt a new interpretation of scripture. Similarly the death and resurrection of Christ resulted in the Church's transformation of the liturgy of the synagogue. Moreover, the paraliturgy or domestic rites of the Jewish home in the observance of the Sabbath and Passover became, through Christ's institution of the eucharist at the Last Supper, the heart and centre of the life of the Church. In the commemoration of Christ's sacrifice the Church celebrates her redemption.

Since the eucharistic liturgy was absolutely central to the existence and faith of the Church, it followed that it began to be extended to the whole of its life. From at least the middle of the second century, and probably earlier, it was associated with the rite of entry into the Church. Once the Church, independently of the synagogue, began to spread into the pagan world, a rite of initiation was necessarily developed. From the time of St Paul, it was invested with the character of Christ's death and resurrection. Converts to Christ were, paradoxically, 'baptised into His death'. Through His death they 'died' to their old worldly existence, and in union with Him in His resurrection 'walked in newness of life'. The preparation of converts for baptism did much to map out the season of Lent, and baptism itself was more and more associated with the Christian Passover feast of Easter. Before baptism, converts were freely admitted to that part of the Christian liturgy which was directly derived from the synagogue. But such converts were dismissed from the church before the beginning of the eucharistic liturgy. It was only after they had undergone the rite of initiation that they were admitted to the domestic privacy of, and to that which was innermost in, the life of the Church. The initiation at the Easter vigil reached its climax in the celebration of the eucharist as Easter day began to dawn. Christians no longer lived (in the phrase of St Ignatius) 'in accordance with Judaism', but 'in accordance with Christ Jesus'. They began to live out in their lives all the implications of eucharistic worship.

Like initiation, ordination was directly associated with the eucharist. Distinctions within the institutional life of the Church were, as we know from the letters of St Paul, evident from the first. The range of 'ministries' was manifold. But in time these were rooted in the liturgical life of the Church, so that the structure of the Church was intimately related to its liturgy. Among the many duties of the bishop is the offering of the gifts in the eucharist. Indeed, the earliest extant text of the ordination liturgy, that of *The Apostolic Tradition*, provided that the bishop, straightway after his ordination by the laying on of hands by other bishops, shall

> offer the gifts . . . and when he has been made bishop let everyone offer him the kiss of peace . . . To him then let the deacons bring the oblation, and he with all the presbyters laying his hand on the oblation shall give thanks.

Then follows the eucharistic prayer. The presbyters 'concelebrate' with the bishop, having no distinct liturgy of their own. In course of time, however, since the bishop could not be everywhere at once, it was to them that he delegated the celebration of the eucharistic sacrifice; thus they came to share in the priesthood of the bishop. The deacons, for their part, had a primary duty to serve the Lord's table.

Eventually the rites of passage through life, marriages and funerals, also came to be consecrated by being drawn into the eucharistic liturgy. Marriage is solemnised by the Church, first by bringing the married couple into the eucharistic liturgy for blessing (thus relating marriage to the work of redemption), and later by incorporating the marriage rite itself into the eucharist. In the case of death, it was evidently the practice from at least the third and fourth centuries for Christians to receive the eucharist before dying, as a means of assuring them a part in the eternal Easter of Christ. Later the funeral rite itself was directly associated with the celebration of the liturgy of the eucharist.

THE LITURGY OF TIME

Christian liturgy, so far considered, is focused upon the sacrifice of Christ. The effects of Christ's work of salvation are transmitted to those taking part in the liturgy. But there is another extension of Christian liturgy, of a non-sacramental kind – namely, the liturgy of time. In this the day, the week, the season and the year are sanctified by a ceaseless round of prayer. Here again, the inspiration for the Church's hours of prayer was the daily evening and morning liturgy of the synagogue. The evening and morning services of the synagogue were matched in the Church by Vespers, and Matins with Lauds, respectively. It is particularly striking that Psalm 95, the introductory psalm for the evening inauguration of the Sabbath, became the introductory psalm for Matins, the night office of the Church. Eventually the Church introduced the lesser offices of Prime, Terce, Sext, None, and Compline, investing these with the commemoration of the Lord's Passion.

In the Church's daily hours of prayer it is just possible to discern another subtle influence of the synagogue – in the chant. Chant is indigenous to liturgy. Readings from scripture, the use of the psalms, and the prayers both of the officiant and of the congregation were all intoned. The purpose of intonation was complex. It facilitated the punctuation and interpretation of the text; it tended to eliminate idiosyncrasies and to promote objectivity in the treatment of the text; it enabled the congregation to keep together, and the individual voice to carry in large spaces. Intonation therefore served the Church no less than the synagogue, and it appears that some elements of synagogue chant survived in the usage of the Church. Of course, from these remote origins Christian chant has developed in its own way and in accordance with the character of the different languages of the Church.

THE PURPOSE OF LITURGY

The Church's liturgy has a single purpose, yet with a double aspect. Liturgy from one standpoint gives glory to God. It expresses in time the timeless worship of the angelic orders who call to one another, 'Holy, holy, holy, Lord God of hosts; heaven and earth are full of thy glory'. Yet at the same time, from another standpoint, liturgy serves the salvation of man. The sacraments effect in man what they signify; and the Church's daily prayer sanctifies the whole life of man, not only of those who actually participate, but also of those who with them make up the whole Body of Christ.

11

In the eucharistic liturgy Christ is present by virtue of His sacrifice on the Cross. But He is also present in the extension of the Church's liturgy in its various forms, for He is the Word of God speaking in the New Testament and the Old. Christ is present in the priest by virtue of his ordination in the hierarchic structure of the Church, which descends through the centuries from apostolic origins. He is present, too, in and among the people by virtue of their baptism into His death. In the Church's liturgy, therefore, the whole Christ – head and members – offers himself to the Father for His glory.

The Evolution of the Roman Liturgy

Professor David Hiley

Because liturgies reflect the aspirations of the societies in which they evolve, they are never constant in detail or even in design. Although this essay purports to treat of 'the' liturgy, there was really no such thing; instead there was an almost infinite variety of more or less similiar liturgies. Even if one focuses on the Roman liturgy (as opposed to other western rites, such as the Milanese, the Gallican or the Mozarabic, and to the various eastern rites), one has still to reckon with wide variations in practice caused by the different requirements of particular places and periods. For example, the liturgical forms in use during the persecution under Diocletian (284–305) did not answer all the needs of the confident and state-supported church of the later fourth century. Likewise, the eighth-century papal liturgy, transplanted into Frankish lands under Pepin and Charlemagne, did not emerge unmodified by the experience; many new alterations and additions were necessary to make it appropriate for new and local conditions.

The sketch which follows must therefore take account of the changing items which made up the various liturgies and also of the conditions which necessitated them. Some mention should also be made of the sources on which the sketch is based. Service books have survived in a haphazard and uneven fashion, and some areas and periods of liturgical custom are not represented at all. This is particularly true, of course, for the early centuries; we have, for example, no books containing Roman prayers from before the seventh century. It also, however, affects our knowledge of later times, especially in such matters as musical performance practice. Musical notation was not used in the West until the ninth century, when the desire to record 'correct' melodies, thought at the time to have been composed by Pope Gregory the Great (died 604) under divine inspiration, led to the first codification of musical practice.

The role of books in the enactment of holy ritual is itself the subject of debate. Not all the books which have survived would have been sung from during a service. Many are records of a church's use for reference only; this must be true not simply of ordinals, which contain only the opening words of the items in the year's services, but also of many missals, breviaries and the like, which contain compendia of material performed by several different persons. And many early musical manuscripts, such as graduals and tropers, are simply too small to have been read during performance. Many extant books are presentation copies – gifts that were perhaps never used in church, although possibly kept on an altar there. From the thirteenth century, when copies of liturgical books could be commissioned from professional workshops in Paris, Oxford, and elsewhere, books became a popular item for pious men to give to churches. For these and other reasons, the evidence of service books, like any sort of evidence for the development of liturgy through the centuries, has to be evaluated with care.

Rome and its liturgical customs achieved a special position in Christendom at an early date, but it was not the only centre of importance. For instance, it is likely that Antioch, the metropolis of Syria, was the first centre to sing psalmody with two alternating choirs (this kind of antiphonal singing was used in the synagogue and had become popular with some heretical sects, so the Syrian church turned it against them). Introduced at Antioch in the second half of the fourth century, this practice had spread to Jerusalem by 400, and it was in general use in both East and West in the sixth century. Jerusalem, the site of the most holy places of Christendom, led the way in the development of the symbolic cycle of holy days which constitutes the church year, in which the events of the Nativity, the Passion, the Resurrection, the Ascension, and Pentecost were commemorated annually in their proper season. The earliest and most important of all Christian rituals, baptism and the eucharist, were themselves reenactments of crucial events in the Gospels, and so the development of a series of commemorations of events in Jesus's life and ministry sprang from an inherent feature of Christian thought.

Rome, the ancient capital of the empire (and still, after Diocletian's division, the spiritual centre of its western half), had seen the ministry of the apostles, among whom Peter was reckoned as the city's first bishop. But, considering the strong Christian communities of Syria, Palestine, Asia Minor, and Egypt, it is not be to expected that Rome took a decisive lead in every facet of liturgical evolution. Greek, the lingua franca of the empire, was in fact used in the Roman liturgy until the time of Pope Leo I (440-61), and vestiges of it remain in the Kyrie and in the Reproaches on Good Friday. Further eastern elements came into the Roman rite during and immediately after the attempted reconquest of the West by Justinian and his successors in the sixth and seventh centuries. It should also be borne in mind that for several centuries the Rome liturgy was but one of a number of influential western rites. Although some of these were superseded by the customs of Rome quite early on (the Celtic rite disappeared from Britain during the seventh century, and the Gallican rite from the lands of the Franks during the eighth, for example), others survived for much longer. The Ambrosian liturgy of Milan has preserved its independence until the present day. (Programme 8 in this series – see page 63 – presents an Ambrosian Mass of the mid-twelfth century.)

In some respects, however, Rome did influence the rest of Christendom. In the early centuries Christmas had been a commemoration of both the Nativity and the Baptism of Our Lord, and had been celebrated on 6 January, the date of the winter solstice established by Egyptian astronomers at the beginning of the second millennium BC. It is from Rome, in the early fourth century AD, that we first have evidence that the Nativity was being celebrated on 25 December. The old date of the solstice was no longer accurate, and in 274 the Emperor Aurelian had declared 25 Decem-

14

ber (the correct date) to be the festival of the Invincible Sun. Christians in Rome must have followed suit in commemorating their own 'Sun of Righteousness' on the same day. By 380 Constantinople had adopted the custom from Rome, leaving 6 January as the baptismal feast. At Antioch in 386 John Chrysostom celebrated the Nativity for the first time on 25 December, saying 'it is not yet the tenth year since this day has become clearly known to us...which has been known from of old to the inhabitants of the West'. Here, then, a custom originating in Rome prevailed elsewhere.

The toleration of Christianity under Constantine I and its adoption as the religion of the Empire under Theodosius I (379–95) must have had an enormous effect on all aspects of the life of the church, not least on the development of its ritual. Congregations increased in size; benefactions for the building and furnishing of churches were made openly and with the approval of society; the array of ornaments, vessels and vestments was enriched; ceremonial became more elaborate; and a sense of awe at the divine mystery of the eucharist was inculcated. It is instructive to compare the description of the Roman eucharist written in *c.* 150 by Justin Martyr with the ornate ritual expounded in *c.* 410 by Theodore of Mopsuestia (who had been trained at Antioch). Justin wrote to show pagans that Christian rites were not black magic. He describes a simple, straightforward liturgy containing readings from the 'memoirs of the apostles' and from the prophets; the bishop preached a sermon; there followed a solemn prayer and the kiss of peace; and the bishop offered thanks for the sacred elements which were then distributed by deacons to the faithful (both to those who were present and to those who were sick or in prison). Although the penalty might be death, it was a sacred duty for every Christian to attend each Sunday meeting.

With Theodore we are in a very different world. For example, a solemn procession is made at the bringing of the bread and wine to the altar; the deacons spread linen cloths on the altar, representing those of Christ's burial; they 'fan' the Body on the altar, thereby personifying the winged angels who kept watch over Christ's passion and death. There is a continual insistence on the awesome nature of the rite: 'Because the Body lying there is a high, dreadful, holy and true Lord, through its union with the divine nature, it is with great fear that it must be seen and kept.' It must be admitted that the elaboration of ritual proceeded faster and further in the East than in the West during the fourth century, but the change in style is everywhere evident; it is a change dictated by the development of an illegal and private ritual into a state-supported and public one. Nor was ceremonial alone affected: the *Apostolic Constitutions* of the late fourth century show that eucharistic prayers were being codified (where previously they had been improvised), and that such prayers were often of great prolixity (as they continued to be in, for example, the Gallican rite).

Just as the year came to be filled with commemorations of events in the lives of our Lord and the saints, so there arose the custom of performing the liturgy on days other than Sundays and commemorations. Christian worship took place not on the Jewish Sabbath (the seventh day of the week), but on the first day of the week, and this must have been so from a very early date (see Acts 20:7 and I Corinthians 16:2). By the second century many individuals fasted on Wednesdays and Fridays, the days of Christ's betrayal and crucifixion (the Pharisaic custom had been to fast on Mondays and Thursdays). By the fourth century Saturday (the old Sabbath) was also frequently solemnised in this way, despite protests at a 'Judaizing' tendency. With fasting might go communion. Thus in 372 St Basil wrote: 'It is good and beneficial to communicate every day...I, indeed, communicate four times a week, on the Lord's day, on Wednesday, on Friday, and on the Sabbath, and on the other days if there is a commemoration of any saint.'

As the celebration of the eucharist spread from Sunday to other days, so other services joined the eucharist, to fill each day with liturgical acts of one type or another. These were naturally the concern not so much of lay Christians as of those dedicated to the religious life: bishops and their households, priests and other clergy, and also the numerous ascetics living in the vicinity of the town churches. (From the late fourth century onwards such ascetics showed an increasing tendency to establish monastic communities out of town, in the seclusion of the countryside or the desert.) Information about the actual content of formal acts of worship other than Mass in the early centuries is more or less non-existent. The first surviving descriptions concern fourth-century Jerusalem, about whose practice we are informed by the aristocratic Gaulish pilgrim Egeria (Etheria, or Sylvia). She describes a daily cycle of services at the church of the Anastasis in Jerusalem (the church of the Holy Sepulchre, which was one of the secondary churches at that time).

It was probably services rather similar to these that St Benedict (c. 480–547) would have known in his youth in Rome and during his years as an anchorite at Subiaco, when he acted as spiritual advisor to several local monastic communities. When in 529 he founded a monastery at Monte Cassino, he provided it with a 'Rule' that came to dominate western monasticism for centuries. The order of worship laid down by Benedict describes a nocturnal office followed by a morning service at daybreak; then there are four day services, Prime, Terce, Sext, and None; and in the evening come Vespers and Compline, the latter being a brief act of prayer for safe repose. Thus the Benedictine monk could say with the prophet, 'Seven times in the day have I given praise to Thee.' This cycle of daily devotions became known as the Divine Office.

During the first five or six centuries the chief components of the Mass (leaving aside the essential celebration of the eucharist) and the Divine Office fell into three categories: prayers, readings from scripture, and psalmody (the singing of psalms and canticles). Despite later accretions and developments this basic core has remained intact, as Edward Barnes's detailed account of the services in the next essay illustrates.

16

The singing of poetic and non-scriptural texts has rarely been accepted unreservedly in the Roman liturgy. Yet hymn-singing, the most obvious example of such a procedure, had been practised by the very earliest Christians. It is likely, for instance, that such passages as Revelation 15:3–4 quote hymns actually used in the early church:

> Great and marvellous are thy works, Lord God almighty; just and true are thy ways, thou king of saints. Who shall not fear thee, O Lord, and glorify thy name? For thou only art holy: for all nations shall come and worship before thee; for thy judgements are made manifest.

It is also likely that both simple choral hymns and more elaborate solo ones existed, as well as hymns with and without refrains and hymns performed antiphonally. But dancing and hand-clapping, features of the worship of many heretical sects, were forbidden. Towards the end of the third century there were moves to suppress hymns in favour of psalms; the fourth century, however, saw a resurgence of hymn writing with the activities of St Ambrose of Milan (*c.* 339–97), St Hilary of Poitiers (*c.* 315–67), and St Ephrem of Antioch (died 373). But whereas vast quantities of hymns were eventually written for some of the eastern churches (the number of Byzantine hymns exceeds a hundred thousand), and hymns have remained a prominent feature of the Milanese liturgy, the Roman church has generally been conservative in accepting them into regular use.

The authority and prestige that the Roman church gradually acquired in the West did not prevent individual centres from striking out on original paths. We might say that just as the constant need to respond to new conditions caused Rome itself to diverge from the other main churches of Christendom, so local usage within the Roman sphere evolved peculiarities of liturgy which reflected local conditions. For example, the anniversary of a local saint might be celebrated with a full Office and Mass in a certain place, when in Rome itself the day in question would pass unnoticed. Solemn processions would be designed with the geographical placement and plan of local churches and other sites in mind. Churches also frequently differed from each other in the choice of text (whether a prayer, a reading, or a chant) to be used on a particular occasion. Scholars still argue, for instance, about the interrelationships between the various collections of prayers for Mass which have survived from the fourth to the ninth centuries; these show continually shifting crosscurrents caused by new collections (coming from Rome itself) replacing or being conflated with non-Roman (south or north Italian, Gallic, Spanish, Germanic, or English) compilations. For pieces such as hymns, where Roman authority was simply non-existent, the divergence in practice between local churches was particularly wide.

One striking example of this diversity may be seen in the surviving collections of sequences. The Sequence was a hymn sung on feast days before the Gospel; it evolved in the Frankish dominions of Charlemagne and his descendants, but was apparently not at first used at Rome. Probably because the genre lacked the authority of Roman tradition, local cantors seem to have felt relatively free to compose new words to old melodies or to write completely new pieces. By the end of the Middle Ages there were well over five thousand sequences in existence. Because of their non-scriptural nature they were frowned upon by the Council of Trent, and their popularity declined rapidly thereafter.

The production of new material for use within the general framework of the Roman liturgy was particularly exuberant after the establishment of Roman use in the Frankish empire under Pepin (reigned 751–71) and Charlemagne (reigned 771–814). Sequences were produced in great quantity in this region. In the ninth and tenth centuries it also became customary in several influential churches (such as the Abbey of St Gall in Switerland) to 'gloss' certain types of chant – principally the Introit, or entrance chant at Mass. Such glosses were called tropes; they consisted of short phrases of new text and music sung by soloists between the phrases of the original chant. The new text usually commented on or expanded the original one, as the beginning of the troped Gloria below demonstrates; the words of the trope are printed in italics (the complete piece can be heard in Programme 10):

> Glory be to God in the highest, *whose glory resounds in all the world*. And on earth peace, *perpetual peace*, to men of good will, *who truly love God*.

Words were also frequently added (according to the principle of one syllable per note) to the lengthy vocalisations often found in solo chants, such as the Alleluia, Offertory, and responsory melismas; examples of this kind of trope, which was known as a prosula, can be heard in several programmes in this series. Many collections of tropes, prosulae, and allied forms survive from between about 900 and 1200; thereafter such material seems generally to have gone out of fashion, although there were areas (such as England) where the tradition lived on.

Among other medieval accretions to the liturgy, there is space here to mention only the liturgical drama. Since the eucharist itself is essentially a reenactment of the Last Supper, and since the cycle of holy days between Christmas and Whitsun is an annual commemoration of actual events, it can be argued that there is an implicitly dramatic element in Christian ritual. In Carolingian times there developed a brief ceremonial reenactment, with singers representing the biblical personages, of the visit of the three Marys to the empty tomb and the angel's news of Christ's resurrection. In the eleventh century the other events of Eastertide were incorporated in greatly expanded reenactments of this sort, and the Christmas story and other events from the Bible and the lives of saints received the same treatment.

The increasing number and elaboration of the ceremonial actions accompanying the liturgy, which begin to be evident during the fourth century when Christian worship became public, were much more characteristic of the Syrian and other eastern churches than of the Roman church, whose ritual usually retained a distinct directness of character. Some of the most obvious features of Roman ceremonial are ancient, while others are not. In the beginning, for example, officiating ministers wore the normal clothes of persons on formal business rather than special and splendid vestments; as the centuries passed, other fashions changed but clerical dress did not, and thus it acquired a ceremonial character almost by accident. The mitre is an addition of the eleventh century, while the cope and gloves appeared some two hundred years earlier; and the last two originated in France rather than in Rome. Again, the altar remained bare of cross, candles, books or any other decorative or symbolic objects until the Carolingian era. The burning of incense, on the other hand, was common from the beginning (see Revelation 5:8 and 8:3–4), and had become universal by the fifth century. Pictures and statues have always been present in churches within the Roman sphere, but they were not involved in liturgical acts until the increased veneration of the Blessed Virgin in and after the thirteenth century.

In the twentieth century, scholars of liturgy have tended to concentrate on the early and medieval church. Yet in view of the constantly changing character of Christian worship it cannot cause surprise that liturgies have continued to develop up to our own day. In the Renaissance, books radically revised on humanist lines were briefly fashionable: books such as the *Breviary of the Holy Cross* of Cardinal Quiñonez, published in 1535, in which many texts were completely replaced and some services were even altered in structure. Fortunately, the Council of Trent (1542–63) did not adopt a radical attitude towards the ancient texts; Quiñonez's versions were not perpetuated, and only late medieval material (some of it accumulated during the Avignon exile) was suppressed. The reformed Roman breviary of 1568 and the missal of 1570 would not, therefore, have alarmed a medieval precentor. With the music, however, it was different. Chant was drastically revised according to humanist concepts of word-setting and contemporary ideas about tonality, first by Palestrina and Annibale Zoilo, then by Guidetti, and finally by Anerio and Soriano (the composer of the polyphony in Programme 9), whose new book of chants appeared in 1614–15. Another wave of reform swept France in the seventeenth and eighteenth centuries, chiefly for political and anti-papal reasons; the words and music of the liturgy were radically revised in many dioceses as a means of asserting the independence of the French church.

At the same time, the late Renaissance saw the beginning of scholarly work which would eventually facilitate a return to original texts. Editions of ancient books and studies of liturgical customs were partly a reaction to the wholesale jettisoning of traditional material that marked the 'editions' of the sixteenth, seventeenth, and eighteenth centuries. Thus Pamelius in late sixteenth-century France, Thomassin and Mabillon in France and Tomasi in Italy in the seventeenth century, and the Belgian Martene in the eighteenth century, all provided editions and studies which were used by the 'Ultramontane' movement in nineteenth-century France, when the pendulum swung the other way.

The task of restoring chant to its original state was accomplished much less easily. Here the question was not simply of returning to Roman use, because the official

Roman chant books themselves contained the corruptions of the sixteenth and seventeenth centuries. The first major steps in the plainchant revival were taken in 1851, when an eleventh-century manuscript from Dijon was used as the basis of a gradual published for the dioceses of Rheims and Cambrai, and when a pseudo-facsimile (actually containing many errors and omissions) of a tenth-century St Gall manuscript was published by Lambilotte. The campaign for a return to authentic chant forms lasted for half a century; indeed, one could say that it is not over now. Largely as a result of the work of Dom Joseph Pothier and the monks of the Benedictine Abbey of Solesmes, restored chant books were sanctioned by Pope Pius X and published in 1905 (the Ordinary of the Mass), 1908 (the Proper of the Mass), and 1912 (the chants of the Divine Office). Ever since, the scholars of Solesmes have been at the forefront of chant research.

   After further reform in recent decades, the use of these restored books is itself no longer obligatory. The nineteenth- and twentieth-century restoration of medieval chant may, perhaps, be seen as an eccentric twist in the continuous evolution of liturgical practice from the earliest days of Christianity. Like every other event in the history of the liturgy, however, it answered a contemporary need, and in promoting a deeper understanding of the past it has enriched both the present and the future of our civilisation.

The Development of the Mass and the Divine Office

Edward Barnes

This account deals mainly with the Roman rite and the local uses derived from it. The only rite of separate origin to be noticed is that of Milan (called Ambrosian), whose Mass will be heard in Programme 8 of this series, on 30 December. The major differences between the Roman and Milanese masses will be described later. Furthermore, we are concerned only with High Mass (which has a full complement of servers, a subdeacon and a deacon to read the lessons, and a choir to sing the chants) and not with Low Mass (which is celebrated by a single priest who speaks all of the texts, assisted by a server who says the responses).

The Mass divides naturally into two parts: the synaxis, or Mass of the Catechumens (now somethimes called 'the liturgy of the Word'), and the eucharist itself, the Mass of the Faithful, which begins with the Offertory. This division is as old as the Mass itself; originally the two parts were separable, and up to the fifth century it was quite normal to perform one part without the other. From the Middle Ages to the present day, the synaxis has never ceased to be regarded as a prelude to the eucharist: he who is not present for the whole of the latter has not heard Mass.

The synaxis was derived from the service of the synagogue, and until the fourth century (when Christian worship became public rather than private, and expanded and diverged) it was essentially the same all over Christendom. It began with the celebrant's greeting and the congregation's reply. Readings followed, usually three in number, from the Old Testament, the apostolic writings, and the Gospels. Between the readings psalms were sung, usually responsorially (the main methods of psalmody or psalm-singing are described below). After the Gospel reading came the officiant's sermon. Those who had not yet been admitted into full church membership were then dismissed. (This is the moment when, in the Byzantine rite, the formal instruction 'The doors, the doors' is still given.) Prayers for the needs of all men were then said by the officiant and the faithful. The eucharist followed, or if the eucharist was not to be celebrated the faithful were dismissed.

The singing of psalms was an important constituent of the early synaxis. Later on it became less prominent as other items were added, and the psalms were curtailed or discarded to make room for them. Psalms and canticles did, however, continue to form the backbone of the Divine Office, as we shall see. There were two main methods of singing psalms: responsorial or solo psalmody, and antiphonal or choral psalmody. Responsorial psalmody was the older of the two and was adopted from synagogue practice. The psalm was recited or sung by a soloist, the congregation being silent, or responding with 'alleluia' after each verse, or responding with re-frains either taken from the psalm itself or newly composed. In the West, complete psalms ceased to be performed in this way at an early date; the main survivals, each having not more than one or two psalm verses and perhaps the Gloria Patri as well, are the responsories of Matins (see Programme 1) and processions (see Programmes 3, 4 and 7), and the Gradual and Alleluia of Mass. The Alleluia is treated as responsorial psalmody, although it probably consisted originally of the word 'alleluia' alone, to which the psalm verse was later added.

In contrast, solo singers had no role in choral or antiphonal psalmody, in which two choral groups sang in alternation. (This method of singing is also known as *alternatim* performance.) The origins of antiphonal psalmody are uncertain, but it was already familiar to St Basil (329–70), whose monastic 'Rule' has been for the East what that of St Benedict has been for the West. At an early stage choral refrains were introduced between the verses; these, rather confusingly, were known as antiphons, so that antiphonal psalmody came to signify not only the alternation of two choral groups but also the presence of an 'antiphon' refrain. By the early Middle Ages it was customary to sing the refrain only at the beginning and end of the psalm, and the first statement often came to be abbreviated still further, so that only its first few words were sung. The psalms of the Divine Office were and still are performed in this fashion (see Programme 1). Antiphonal psalmody had, however, almost completely disappeared from the Mass by the end of the first millennium. This came about in two ways. First, the introduction of new items led to the shortening of what had previously been antiphons with several psalm verses by omitting most or all of the verses ; this is what happened in the Introit, Offertory, and Communion. Second, at an unknown date the remaining psalm verses were either shared between the choir and solo singers (as in the Introit) or completely taken over by soloists (as in the Offertory). This could lead to their becoming very elaborate – as, for example, in the Offertory verse in Programme 10. A third and minor form of psalmody may be mentioned at this point. In direct psalmody the psalm or part of it is simply sung or recited straight through without any additional text; this survives in the Mass only in the Tract, which replaces the Alleluia during Lent.

In the Roman rite the synaxis reached its medieval (and in most respects, modern) form through the omission or shortening of some items and the adoption of others. Thus the intercessory prayers after the sermon disappeared around the year 500 (although they have survived on Good Friday), and the sermon itself became optional. The Old Testament lesson was retained only on special occasions. The Introit (an entrance-psalm with antiphon) was introduced but soon lost most of its verses. A litany, later condensed into the Kyrie, and a hymn of praise, the Gloria, were inserted before the celebrant's greeting, and a prayer or Collect after it. The last major addition was the Credo, which was adopted at Rome early in the eleventh century and which follows the Gospel.

Before setting out in order the events of the Mass, it will be useful to examine the development of the eucharist itself. The eucharist is built round four actions: the offertory, in which bread and wine are taken and offered at the altar; the eucharistic prayer, in which the celebrant gives thanks over the bread and wine (which are often called the 'oblations'); the fraction, when the bread is broken; and the communion, when the Body and Blood are distributed. Before the fourth century the eucharist consisted simply of these four elements, preceded by a greeting and the kiss of peace. At Rome it reached its later shape by the relocation of the kiss of peace at a point before the communion and by the addition of several items. These included the Lord's Prayer, inserted immediately after the eucharistic prayer, so that it was treated as part of it: choral psalms with antiphons to accompany the offertory and the communion (these soon lost most or all of their psalm verses); a prefatory prayer and the Sanctus before that part of the eucharistic prayer which is called the Canon; the Agnus Dei to accompany the fraction; and various private devotions of the celebrant and servers.

One further practical point should be made. The more extensive and complicated the ritual and musical elements became, the more essential it was to have a competent official in charge of them. The office of cantor (in English usage, precentor) was an ancient one, taken over from the synagogue by the early church; its incumbent was ultimately responsible for the correct performance of the liturgy and its music. Before the service he or his deputy, the succentor, would make sure that everybody knew what was to be sung and would decide who should sing the solo chants. During the service he would intone (begin) the choral chants himself, so that the pitch was set before the choir came in; or intimate the correct intonation to one or two pairs of senior singers called rulers, who stood between the two sets of stalls and who led the choir on major feasts. He also ensured that the celebrant began the Gloria and Credo with the right intonation and at a suitable pitch, and he set the pitch for the solo chants. By no means least important, he directed the chanting with a system of gestures known as cheironomy. When polyphony began to be sung, its supervision was as first usually entrusted to the cantor, but by the fourteenth century it was tending to become the responsibility of another member of the choir, whose duties gradually evolved into those of the master or instructor of the choir of later times.

THE ROMAN MASS IN THE LATER MIDDLE AGES

The items of Mass divide into two categories, according to whether or not their texts change from day to day. Those which have texts that change are known as the Proper, and the others are known as the Ordinary. The main items of the Proper are the Introit, Collect, Epistle, Gradual, Alleluia, Sequence, Gospel, Offertory, Secret, Preface, Communion, and Postcommunion.

Mass begins with the Introit (*antiphona ad introitum*), which accompanies the entrance of the celebrant and his assistants, their preparatory prayers at the altar (probably introduced during the eleventh century) and the censing of the altar (which continues during the Kyrie). The Introit consists of antiphon–psalm verse–Gloria Patri–antiphon. Originally (perhaps in the fifth century) there were several psalm verses or possibly even a complete psalm, each verse being followed by a repetition of the antiphon; and a relic of this persisted in the additional repetition of the antiphon between the verse and the Gloria Patri in Norman-French and English medieval uses. The psalm verse and Gloria Patri are sung to simple melodic formulae called psalm tones.

The Introit is followed by the Kyrie, a ninefold invocation to the Father, Son, and Holy Spirit, borrowed by Rome from the eastern church (probably in the sixth century) and retaining the original Greek text. From the ninth century onwards, the melismata of the Kyrie chants were often supplied with prosulae or added words to make them relevant to particular occasions or circumstances. Examples of Kyrie prosulae can be heard in Programmes 1, 4, 7, and 10.

The Gloria, which follows the Kyrie, was also taken over by Rome from Byzantium, probably in the seventh century. It is not sung on ordinary weekdays, in Advent, or from Septuagesima to Easter, so its reappearance on Christmas Day and Easter Day enhances the festal nature of those occasions. It is the first of the two choral chants to be intoned by the celebrant, the Credo being the other.

After the Gloria the celebrant turns towards the congregation (a term which includes the choir and any others present) and salutes them, the congregation making a simple response. The usual greeting is 'Dominus vobiscum', and the reply, 'Et cum spiritu tuo'. If the celebrant is a bishop he says 'Pax vobis' instead. The salutation is where the synaxis originally began. The celebrant will salute the congregation five times during the Roman mass; in the Ambrosian Mass he salutes them no fewer than ten times.

The celebrant now recites the prayer called the Collect, which has a text apposite to the day. It is recited to a monotone with simple inflections at the main grammatical divisions, and is concluded with a conventional textual formula. If a major feast has recently been celebrated there may now follow a memorial or Commemoration of it, consisting of its own Collect. Most English uses, for example, stipulate that on 29 December the Collect of St Thomas of Canterbury should be followed by four Memorials or Commemorations, the Collects of the Nativity, St Stephen, St John, and the Holy Innocents (see Programme 7).

After the Collect and commemorations there are in most of the western uses two readings, the Epistle (or another portion of Scripture in its place) and the Gospel. Each is chanted to a reading tone, with inflections at the main grammatical divisions, partly so that they shall be heard distinctly and partly to give them solemnity. The Epistle is read by a subdeacon and the Gospel by a deacon, both usually in a high place, either (as often in England and northern Europe) from the pulpitum above the quire screen, or (as in southern France, Italy, and Iberia) from a raised pulpit or gallery on the wall of the quire or sanctuary. On a few occasions, such as Christmas Eve and Christmas Day in the English uses, there is an extra Old Testament lesson (called a Prophecy) before the Epistle.

Between the Epistle and Gospel come the Gradual (*responsorium graduale*), the

Alleluia, and sometimes the Sequence. The Gradual was at one time a complete psalm with a refrain, but by the early Middle Ages all that remained was the refrain (or responsory) itself and a single psalm verse, both sung to elaborate melodies that demanded virtuoso singing. Although it was treated as a responsory, the Alleluia probably evolved in the opposite direction, originating as a lengthy melismatic treatment of the single word 'alleluia', to which a psalm verse was subsequently added. In Lent and on other penitential occasions the Alleluia is replaced by the Tract, a number of psalm verses sung in direct psalmody. In Eastertide a second Alleluia replaces the Gradual.

During the eighth and ninth centuries it seems to have been customary to lengthen still further the already extensive melisma on the final syllable of the word 'alleluia'. (It is possible that the *melodiae* of the Alleluia in the Ambrosian liturgy arose in the same way at roughly the same time.) Soon afterwards, texts called pro-sulae were added to these melsimata, which consequently acquired an identity of their own and became detached from their parent Alleluias. Thus was born the Sequence, which follows the Alleluia on feast days in most of the medieval uses. Many sequences have a characteristic form, in which pairs of stanzas identical in metre and rhyme are each sung to double statements of different melodic units.

After the Sequence a deacon greets the congregation and reads the Gospel, the dignity of which is emphasised by the lighted candles and incense which accompany the reader. In some uses the celebrant delivers an audible blessing before the read-ing, but only very rarely is there a congregational thanksgiving afterwards. A ser-mon may now be preached but is not obligatory.

On ordinary days and minor feasts the synaxis ends at this point. On Sundays and greater feasts the Nicene Creed (Credo) is sung, being intoned by the celebrant and continued by everybody. Although it was in use in the Frankish lands in the late eighth century, this was one of the latest additions to the Roman liturgy, finally ac-cepted only in the early eleventh century.

The celebrant begins the eucharist by saluting the congregation for the second time. The offertory follows, in which he offers the bread and wine at the altar, say-ing certain invariable private prayers introduced into the western rites during the tenth and eleventh centuries. He then censes the oblations and the altar, and all pre-sent are censed in descending order of seniority. Meanwhile the antiphon known as the Offertory (*antiphona ad offertorium*) is sung. Like the other Proper chants of the Mass which accompany an action, this is an example of antiphonal psalmody, although the melodies are more ornate than those of the Introit and Communion. The Offertory retained one or two psalm verses rather longer than the other Proper chants did (until the early fourteenth century, and even later in England on certain days), and these verses were as lengthy and elaborate as the antiphons themselves (see Programme 2). The Offertory was allowed to attain this size and complexity for a practical reason: originally it accompanied the presentation of bread and wine at the chancel rail by the laity. (This survives in a modified form in the offering of the *vecchioni* in the Ambrosian Mass.) When this practice ceased, the Offertory was soon curtailed by the omission of its verses.

After the censing and the offertory the celebrant washes his hands and says silently the variable offertory prayer called the Secret (*Secreta*); the name may originally have signified 'the mysteries' and have referred to the eucharistic prayer into which the Secret leads. The doxology or conclusion of this Secret is said aloud to prepare the congregation for the beginning of the eucharistic prayer.

The celebrant now salutes the congregation for the third time and initiates the short dialogue, 'Lift up your hearts' (*Sursum corda*), that leads into the Preface. The Preface, which is chanted by the celebrant, forms an introduction to the Sanctus. For most of the year its text does not change, but there are special prefaces for important days and seasons.

The Sanctus follows at once. This was another import from Byzantium which had probably entered the Roman rite by the early fifth century. The Benedictus was added to it slightly later. Originally the Sanctus was sung by everybody, but by the later Middle Ages it was usually sung by the choir alone, leaving the Credo as the only truly congregational chant.

After the Sanctus the celebrant continues the eucharistic prayer, saying silently that part of it called the Canon. The name probably refers to the sacrosanct and inviolable nature of the prayers of the Canon (which in Latin means a rule or discipline); these prayers were standardised at a very early date and were not subsequently changed. During the Canon the celebrant speaks the words of Jesus at the Last Supper and elevates the Host and (by the sixteenth century) the chalice.

The celebrant announces the end of the Canon by chanting the final words of its last doxology aloud. We now come to the prayers and actions preparatory to communion. The first of these is the Lord's Prayer (*Pater noster*), chanted by the celebrant and followed by the Embolism, a silent prayer in which the celebrant extends the sense of the final petition of the *Pater noster*. During it he makes the fraction.

The conclusion of the Embolism is chanted aloud. The celebrant then announces the *Pax*, or kiss of peace, which he gives to the assisting deacon. In a Pontifical Mass the bishop now gives a blessing. The final musical item of the Ordinary, the Agnus Dei, is sung at this point; it was introduced in about 700 to accompany the fraction. Meanwhile the kiss of peace is communicated to all in quire, and the celebrant says certain invariable private prayers in preparation for communion.

The communion now takes place, accompanied by the antiphon called Communuion (*antiphona ad communionem*). By the later Middle Ages this antiphon had, at least on most occasions, lost all its psalm verses; in some cases it may never have had any. After the communion the celebrant salutes the congregation and recites the Postcommunion prayer (a brief thanksgiving). He then takes his leave of the congregation in a last salutation, the deacon announces the end of Mass in the Dismissal ('Ite missa est'), and the celebrant and assistants return to the sacristy.

From the late sixteenth century in the Roman rite the celebrant gives an informal blessing after the Dismissal, and before leaving the altar he recites silently the first fourteen verses of St John's gospel. The blessing did not find its way into the English uses, and in them the gospel was recited on the way back to the sacristy.

The differences of detail between the Ambrosian and Roman masses are too numerous to list in full. The most important features are described below.

The celebrant and his assistants enter to the singing of the second *Psallenda* (responsory) from Matins. When they have reached the altar the *Ingressa* is sung; this is an antiphon without a psalm. The Gloria follows, except in Advent and Lent (in Lent it is replaced by a litany). After the Gloria a threefold Kyrie is sung, and the celebrant greets the congregation and recites the variable *Oratio super populum* (Collect). According to Beroldus, in a Pontifical Mass the greeting is still 'Dominus vobiscum'.

On Sundays and feasts there are three lessons, and before each lesson the celebrant blesses the reader. After the Old Testament lesson the *Psalmellus* (Gradual) is sung, and after the Epistle the Alleluia. There are no sequences, but on the greatest feasts there is an antiphon before the Gospel (*antiphona ante evangelium*). After the Gospel a salutation, a threefold Kyrie, and an antiphon (*antiphona post evangelium*) conclude the synaxis.

The eucharist begins with the deacon's proclamation 'Pacem habete' (indicating where the kiss of peace used to be before it was moved to the Roman position). The celebrant chants the variable prayer over the corporal cloth (*oratio super sindonem*). The offertory follows; in some masses the Offertory antiphon (*antiphona ad offerendam*) has verses. The Credo follows the offertory. The variable offertory prayer (*oratio super oblatam*) is chanted aloud after the Credo.

Each Mass has its own Proper Preface. The Canon differs slightly from the Roman one. The fraction, accompanied by a variable antiphon called *Confractorium* (the Agnus Dei is sung only in masses for the dead) precedes the *Pater noster*, and the kiss of peace follows it. Mass ends with a formula of dismissal used also in the Office, and includes a triple threefold Kyrie as at the conclusion of the synaxis. Finally the celebrant chants a blessing.

Psalmody fulfilled different roles in the Mass and the Divine Office. In the former, selected verses from the psalms were used to comment on the readings and to accompany actions with chants suitable to the day or feast. In the latter, complete psalms were recited 'in course': that is, in the order in which they occur in the Old Testament (with certain exceptions). The recitation of the psalter formed the core of the Office.

The Latin word *officium* means a service which one does for another – in this context, one's daily devotion to God. In medieval England the word *servicium* was customarily used instead, and, confusingly, *officium* usually meant the Introit of Mass. In the following description 'Office' always means Divine Office.

The Office originated in the monastic movement of the fourth century. There had been, at least as early as the beginning of the third century, a regime of private prayer by Christians in their homes at midnight, at cockcrow, on rising, at the third, sixth, and ninth hours of the day, and on going to bed; and this regime had included spiritual reading. But it was among congregations of hermits in the desert that the recitation of the psalter 'in course' began. In about 330 St Pachomius first organised it as a corporate exercise for Egyptian monks. Its transference to secular churches was brought about by confraternities of lay ascetics living in the world but imposing on themselves a semi-monastic discipline. These were responsible for a great increase in the pratice of private nocturnal prayer. In 347–8 such a confraternity at Antioch began to meet for this exercise in private houses, but the semi-Arian bishop Leontius wished to keep these meetings of the orthdox under his control, and he induced the members to meet in a basilica. The custom of a daily public vigil service, consisting of the monastic devotion of reciting psalms and canticles and listening to readings, was thus established.

The custom spread rapidly, and it is likely that the centre for its diffusion was Jerusalem, which from early in the fourth century attracted large numbers of monks, domestic ascetics and pilgrims who had leisure to attend frequent services. St Cyril became Bishop of Jerusalem in about 350, and the organisation of the daily cycle of offices at Jerusalem described by the Gaulish pilgrim Egeria in 385 must be his work. Egeria's description began with a night office of psalms (and perhaps canticles) with a prayer after each. This led to Lauds at dawn, during which the bishop and clergy entered. The bishop said prayers and blessed the catechumens and the faithful separately, and as he went out he blessed the people individually. During the day, Sext and None were observed; like Lauds, they consisted of psalms. Finally, Vespers took place as the evening lamps were lit; it contained psalms, prayers, and blessings by the bishop. On weekdays in Lent there was also the day office of Terce, which resembled Sext and None. On Sundays the night office was attended by far greater numbers than on weekdays; all the clergy were present, and the bishop read a gospel lesson.

Daily services of this kind became general throughout Christendom in the later fourth century, but for several hundred years there was great variety between the organisation of the Office in different churches. Secular churches were slower than monasteries in adopting the night office and the 'little hours' of Terce, Sext, and None. The daily cycle was further expanded in many monastic communities by the addition of Prime (on rising for the day) in about 400 and Compline (at bedtime) a little later. When at length uniformity was reached, it was largely due to the influence of the Benedictine rule, and especially to the prestige of the monasteries that grew up around the Roman basilicas. As far as music is concerned, it is likely that the singing of psalms antiphonally began to spread from eastern Syria early in the fourth century, superseding the earlier responsorial method as the normal procedure in the Office. It was introduced at Milan by St Ambrose (bishop 374–97) and at Rome by Pope Damasus (366–84).

During the Middle Ages the night office, Matins, developed into the longest and most complex of the offices and the only one to contain a large element of reading. It occupied the hours before dawn and was followed immediately (or after a short interval) by Lauds. At Christmas an exception was made: the first Mass (the Mass at Cockcrow) was inserted between Matins and Lauds, and Matins was begun before midnight to accommodate it. The following description is of Matins as it was conducted according to Salisbury use in the later Middle Ages, but the general pattern was universal in western Europe.

On a feast of any importance Matins consists of an introduction, three nocturns and a conclusion. The introduction is made up of an opening dialogue between officiant and choir, the invitatory with the psalm *Venite exsultemus*, and a hymn. Each nocturn contains three psalms with antiphons; the three psalms are followed by a group of three lessons, each lesson being followed by a responsory. The conclusion consists of the hymn *Te Deum laudamus*, exceptionally preceded by another item (such as a genealogy at Christmas and at Epiphany).

The invitatory is a short chant proper to the day or feast, divided into two halves, the second half often consisting (as on Christmas Night) of the words 'venite adoremus'. The psalm *Venite exsultemus* is divided into six verses including the Gloria Patri. The rulers in silk copes at the choir step begin the invitatory and the choir completes it. On the greatest feasts the rulers sing the whole invitatory and the choir repeats it. The rulers then sing the psalm, the choir repeating the whole invitatory after the odd-numbered verses and its second half after the even-numbered verses. Finally the rulers begin the invitatory again and the choir completes it. This scheme appears to be a survival of the old responsorial method of psalmody.

The two rulers on the duty side of the choir (the side whose weekly turn it is to carry out such tasks) begin the hymn, and the same side of the choir completes the first verse. The next verse is sung by the other side, and so on until the end. Metrical hymns won a place in the Office in different places at different times, often against opposition. St Ambrose introduced them at Milan, but they entered the liturgical Office mainly through monastic rules, especially that of St Benedict; it was Benedict's hymnal that was eventually adopted at Rome, though not until the tenth or eleventh century. The allocation of hymns between the Office services varied enormously up to the Reformation.

With the psalms we reach the essential constituent of the Divine Office. The fundamental intention was to read through the entire psalter, in order, every week. On feasts, however, proper psalms, particularly appropriate to a certain occasion or saint, gradually came into use, and these interrupted the ordered recitation. On feast days each psalm has its own antiphon, whose first few words only are sung before the psalm; the complete antiphon follows the Gloria Patri. Each antiphon is begun by a member of the choir, in descending order of dignity; each psalm is begun by two of the rulers in alternation; the psalms are sung *alternatim*; finally the antiphon to each psalm is begun by the precentor and completed by the choir. After the last psalm and antiphon of each nocturn a versicle is sung by two boys at the choir step. In the first nocturn this is followed by the *Pater noster,* said silently except for the final petition.

Bible-reading as part of the night office goes back to the beginning of monasticism. However, the night office was accepted by secular clergy more reluctantly than Lauds and Vespers were, and this may be why (having remained a largely monastic office for much longer) Matins became the only office with a sizeable amount of reading. The original purpose had been Bible study, hence the readings tended to be continuous passages from the same book and to include biblical commentaries as well as the Bible itself. On feasts proper lessons often interrupted the continuity of the readings (as we have already seen with the psalms). In Christmas Matins, for example, the first nocturn has lessons from Isaiah, the second has sermons by St Isidore of Seville (*c*. 560–636) and Pope Leo the Great (440–61), and the third has commentaries by Pope Gregory the Great (590–604) and the Venerable Bede (*c*. 673–735) on the gospels of the three Christmass masses. The readings are given from the pulpitum above the quire screen, each by a different reader in ascending order of dignity. The first six of them read in their surplices, having taken off their black woollen choir copes; the last three read in silk copes. The officiant blesses each reader before he begins.

Every reading is followed by a responsory. The singing of responsories was prescribed by St Benedict, and Isidore wrote that *responsoria ab Italis longo ante tempore sunt reperta* ('responsories were invented by the Italians a long time ago'). The responsory is one of the survivals of responsorial psalmody, although the texts are frequently taken from sources other than the psalms and usually there is only a single verse. The Matins responsories are among the finest compositions of western liturgy, in both their music and their literature. Probably the best-known today are those of the last three days of Holy Week (often called *Tenebrae* or 'darkness'), particularly in the settings by Victoria. The responsories for Advent are especially fine; those for Christmas form a dramatic commentary on the Nativity. The first two responsories of each nocturn are begun by two soloists and the third by three, in ascending order of dignity, standing in surplices at the quire step. Each responsory is completed by the choir, the soloists sing the verse, and the choir repeats the second half of the responsory again. Great ingenuity is shown in the ways in which the partial repetition follows the verse without doing violence to the sense. Musically the responsories themselves are original compositions, though standard phrases occur in many of them. The verses and Gloria Patri are usually sung to elaborate psalm tones. The responsories of Matins were extensively utilised to provide chants for processions (see Programmes 3, 4, and 7), but when they were used processionally the performance was in most cases entirely choral.

In the Middle Ages it was customary to read the geneaology of Jesus after the third nocturn of Christmas Matins. A deacon, vested and attended as for the Gospel at Mass, asks a blessing from the officiant and proceeds to the pulpitum to perform the reading, taken from St Matthew. The genealogy from St Luke's gospel is read in the same way in Matins of Epiphany.

Matins ends with the *Te Deum*, begun by the officiant and continued *alternatim* by the choir. The *Te Deum* is, like the Gloria, a hymn of praise fashioned after the general literary style of the psalms. It is believed to have been written by Niceta, Bishop of Remesiana (in what is now Yugoslavia) in about 400. It is sung on Sundays and feasts (except during Advent and from Septuagesima to Easter), and was also used on occasions of rejoicing: Henry V ordered it to be sung on the battlefield of Agincourt. On Christmas Night, as soon as the *Te Deum* is finished, the rulers begin the Introit of Mass.

A Constant Liturgy as a Force against Dissolution and Decay

Dr Jerome Roche

What follows is less a reasoned argument than a personal statement by one Roman Catholic confronted by the recent changes that have altered the face of the Catholic liturgy. I speak not as a liturgical historian – I do not have a ready knowledge of the background that will have been contributed elsewhere in this collection of essays – nor especially as a musician, nostalgically lamenting the detrimental effect the changes have had on the maintenance of the Latin musical heritage, nor yet as a kind of aesthete, anxious that a preservation order should be slapped on the traditional Roman Rite of Mass on account of its cultural and historical value. I write, simply, as one wishing to adhere to the truths and therefore the practices of the faith in which I was brought up. The 'therefore' needs explaining: an oft-quoted Latin tag, *Lex orandi, lex credendi*, will help. The traditional Roman Rite of Mass which evolved, was added to (always by way of improvement), and *never* altered in any substance, over a period of many hundreds of years, represents fully and unequivocally the Catholic doctrine of the Mass; the beliefs are enshrined in the manner of praying.

This is not the place to launch a critique of the *Novus Ordo Missae*, the 'New Mass' instituted by Pope Paul VI in 1970; such a critique has been carried out with full documentation by Michael Davies in *Pope Paul's New Mass* (part 3 of a trilogy entitled *Liturgical Revolution*; Augustine Publishing Company, Devon, 1978). Suffice it to say that for me and, I think, for a sizeable minority of Catholics, this is an unsatisfactory rite, capable of interpretations that are contrary to Catholic belief, and it is certainly not a rite which the Fathers of the Second Vatican Council could have envisaged when they discussed liturgical reform. The damage nevertheless has been done; what we now ask is that the traditional rite be granted parity with the new rite, so that the fullness of the old Roman Mass may be celebrated again in our churches rather than in secret.

I have avoided the usual epithet 'Tridentine' for this form of the Mass, because although it dates from 1570 (just after the Council of Trent), it can give rise to misleading implications – such as that the 1570 Missal constituted a type of reform parallel with the recent changes (see *The New Grove* article on the Mass, vol. 11, p. 770). This is not so. What Pope Pius V did in 1570 was to extend the existing Roman form of Mass – the form that in essentials had evolved continuously, without change of direction or doctrinal implication – to the whole of the Western Church. A better designation, therefore, which emphasises the hallowing of tradition (always a hall mark of Catholic practice), is the word 'immemorial' used by some commentators. It is important to recognise that the recent changes to the Mass, involving major alterations and deletions of substance which actually touch on the doctrinal content of the Sacrifice, are wholly out of keeping with the manner in which the Mass evolved until our time.

In other words, the Catholic Church has until now emphatically espoused the idea of 'a constant liturgy as a force against dissolution and decay'. Indeed, the constant liturgy of the Mass has acted as a primary bulwark against heresy of whatever kind. It is necessary to understand that 'constant' does not mean 'static' or 'immobile' – words which, with their pejorative connotation, are unjustly applied to the traditional liturgy by propagandists for the changes. Of course there have been reforms of the rubrics and the calendar, as well as of the Breviary and the Psalter. But these have had the intention of correcting various imbalances that were creeping in and keeping irrelevant accretions under control – never striking at the beautiful flow and symbolism of the liturgy.

Thus my main argument is not mitigated by the obvious differences between all the liturgical celebrations being reconstructed in this series, for the differences are largely those of local usage, tradition and musical elaboration. Nothing that you hear materially affects what is, or would have been, going on at the altar – something that no broadcast reconstruction can truly convey. Such diversity of practice was tolerated by the Church in the past; Pius V exempted those orders or territories whose distinctive liturgical customs were two hundred or more years old from accepting the Missal of 1570, so that but for the Reformation, England would have continued to conduct its worship according to the use of Sarum. We may well ask why such tolerance to established rites was not shown by Paul VI.

Constancy has also, until now, been as characteristic of the Divine Office as it has of the Mass. One may say of the recent revisions of the Breviary and Office that, though doctrinal significance has not been in contention, the essential character of the traditional forms is now only dimly recognisable in the drastically curtailed and impoverished 'Liturgy of the Hours'. Vespers, for example, apart from preserving the Magnificat, seems almost on a level in format and liturgical dignity with one of the Little Hours in the old rite – hardly a change that qualifies the new arrangements to be viewed as reflecting a 'constant liturgy'. Nor can it be claimed that this impoverishment was conceived purely for reasons of practical convenience; there could have been other ways of alleviating the 'burden' of reciting the Office in private. Here again, it is important that the traditional Office should survive as a symbol of the unity between the prayer of the Church today and that of her saints and faithful throughout the ages.

Once this unity is broken, once the liturgy of the Mass and Office ceases to be recognisable in its essentials, even by those martyrs who died for their faith in the distant past, then the timeless, transcendental qualities of the liturgy may give way to permanent revolution and loss of faith. The liturgy becomes less a cult of God than a cult of man, and there is indeed dissolution and decay. In Cardinal Newman's words, 'Rites which the Church has appointed, and with reason – for the Church's authority is from Christ – being long used cannot be disused without harm to our souls' (*Newman against the Liberals*, ed. M. Davies; New York, 1978: pp. 149–50).

A Developing Liturgy in a Developing Society

Nicholas Kenyon

Why should liturgy change? Because man changes. Worship, in the Christian tradition, is not concerned solely with God's transcendence, with his remoteness from
the world. On the contrary, the Christian liturgy celebrates God's activity in our
world: the complex process of prophecy; the life, death and resurrection of Jesus;
and the continuing work of the church. There *are* eternal truths about God; the purpose of a liturgical act is to make these specific at one time, in one place.

It seems to me to be plain, therefore, that we cannot simply adopt the way of talk-
ing, thinking and acting (the external forms) by which any previous generation
articulated its relationship with God. It may be *easier* to take liturgical constructs as
if they were fixed and immutable (as some have wished to do with the form of
Roman Catholic Mass established in 1570 by Pope Pius V in the bull *Quo primum*);
but I fear that to do so is both unrealistic and misguided. It is unrealistic because,
as the rich variety of liturgical reconstructions in this series so tellingly demonstrates, it is absurd to suggest that there was ever one fixed form of Western liturgy
to which all else aspired. The numerous local variants, the different forms practised
by the religious orders, the widely varying ceremonial and the frequent small mod-
ifications to the Roman texts, all show the need to adapt liturgy to circumstances.
It is misguided because, if we abdicate the responsibility to work out our own needs
in worship (sifting what remains valuable in the liturgies of the past from what has
served its purpose and now must change), we become open to the accusation that
our worship is no more than an aesthetic, nostalgic indulgence.

This may seem an exaggerated charge for anyone in the Roman Catholic branch
of Christianity to make, for was not the Catholic liturgical tradition based firmly on
continuity rather than change? In fact, I think that it has been and still is based on
continuity, despite the charges that have been levelled against it in the twenty or so
years since the Second Vatican Council's Constitution on the Liturgy. The problem
(and the reason for the bitterness of the attacks on the Church's liturgical reform)
has been that the essentials of continuity have not been distinguished from inessen-
tials that may change. To read the condemnation that some writers have heaped
upon the Catholic liturgy of recent years, one would think that the whole apparatus
of worship had been dismantled. On the contrary, what was dismantled was the rub-
rical superstructure to which too many unthinkingly clung. The basic framework of
the liturgy, its most historical and most traditional part, has been strengthened. The
word is preached, thanks are given, and Christ's death and resurrection are celebrated in rites which, as the Constitution stipulated, are of a 'noble simplicity'. The
texts can be understood even if what lies behind them never can be (a frequent

35

confusion in the minds of traditionalists who, I suppose, believe that complex modes of expression and ritual acts that cloud the essence of what goes on at Mass help to symbolise this impossibility of understanding).

To be fair, however, there have also been powerful cultural forces active in recent protests against liturgical change. Many of the most vocal objections to the actions of the Catholic Church in the late 1960s came from intelligent and culturally sensitive non-Catholics who felt that a heritage of music and 'beauty' was being thoughtlessly discarded. Unfortunately, the principal reason that the post-Conciliar liturgy as practised in this country had too often to do without fine music was that the professional musicians aligned themselves against change. The Church's documents made clear time and time again that there was a place for choirs, for the repertory of sacred music from the past, and for the skilled performance of music of all kinds in the renewed liturgy. (See the preface to my own *Sing the Mass*, Geoffrey Chapman, 1973.) But because this did not necessarily involve the repetition of all the pieces of polyphony that choirs loved, in the situations to which they had become accustomed, disillusionment set in. The extraordinary unpreparedness of England (and its clergy) for liturgical reform scarcely helped the matter.

But if choirs and choirmasters had been honest with themselves, there was no more than a thousandth part of the great 'treasury of sacred music' that they had previously been able to preserve in the pre-Conciliar liturgy. In three articles in *The Month*, in 1962, Anthony Milner analysed the flimsy basis on which this notion of a corpus of church music depended: it derived from nineteenth-century Italian ideas canonised by Pope Pius X in his *Motu proprio* of 1904. The cause of all the great music written for the liturgy of the Catholic Church is served best by its revival in contexts such as the present series, in performances of the highest professional standard, in liturgical contexts of the greatest precision. The most profound music written in the past will always find a place in contemporary liturgy, because of the unrivalled power with which it communicates the meaning of the words it sets. But unless that music is placed alongside new expressions of faith (so that the 'treasury' is not merely preserved but also, as the Constitution said, 'fostered with great care'), and is used in liturgical celebrations that speak directly to our age, then we will be worshipping not God, but our own past.

Invitatory *Christus natus est*, from Matins on Christmas Eve. Sarum antiphoner, 1519 (Bodleian Library, Arch. Inf. Cupboard D5, f.51v)

Matins and the First Mass of Christmas (The *Missa in Gallicantu*), as they might have been conducted by the Royal Household Chapel of Mary Tudor on Saturday 25 December 1557

In pre-Reformation England the Mass and the Divine Office were conducted in Latin to various local adaptations of the Roman rite. Of these local uses, that of Salisbury was particularly influential and widely followed. Ironically, only seven years after it had been adopted as the sole use for the southern province of the English church, it and the whole Latin rite were swept away in the Protestant 're-forms' of Edward VI. When Edward died without an heir in 1553, he was succeeded by his sister Mary, the older of Henry VIII's two surviving children (Elizabeth being the other). Mary had remained true to her faith throughout the religious convulsions of the previous twenty years; as Queen she quickly returned the English church to communion with Rome and restored the Latin liturgy, though on the whole she was unable to reverse the dissolution of the monasteries. Mary's household chapel became a major force in her attempt to turn back the clock. Its services were held according to Salisbury use; its singers and composers (who included Thomas Tallis, John Sheppard and William Mundy) were among the finest in the land; and its ritual was as elaborate and its music as sumptuous as could be achieved. Certainly its gothic intricacies had little to do with the new spirit of simplicity evident in all the reformed liturgies.

The Roman church emphasised the joyousness of Christmas Day by granting priests (on this day alone) the privilege of celebrating Mass three times; Pope Gregory the Great mentions this in his sermon which is read at Matins. Thus there are three Masses of Christmas: the *Missa in Gallicantu* (Mass at Cockcrow), celebrated soon after midnight and immediately preceded by Matins; the *Missa in Aurora* (Mass at Dawn), celebrated at or soon after daybreak; and the *Missa Magna* (Main Mass), celebrated at about 11 a.m. The texts of each Mass explore a different aspect of Christ's coming: His birth in our souls as the light and word of God, and the establishment and eternity of His kingdom.

The festal aspect of this recreation of Matins and the first Mass is enhanced by the inclusion of polyphony by John Sheppard, a member of Mary's chapel and one of the finest English composers of this or any other period. His Mass *Cantate*, possibly based on a polyphonic composition of the same name which no longer survives, is a large-scale, highly ornate work, well suited to such an occasion as this. (It may be worth noting that the last two psalms of Christmas Matins begin with the word 'Cantate'.) It is written in six parts, which in this performance are taken by high trebles, means (whose compass is like that of mezzo-sopranos), male altos or countertenors (in two groups), tenors and basses. In his settings of the *Te Deum* and two of the Matins responsories Sheppard usually retains the original plainsong as a long-note cantus firmus in the tenor voice, while the rest of the choir creates a luxuriant texture of interwoven counterpoint.

In Mary's chapel these services would have formed a complex ceremony of spectacle and sound, as the priests and clerks performed a series of manoeuvres which were almost a choreographic equivalent to the complicated ordering of the plainchant. For example, at Matins each of the nine psalms with its antiphon was intoned from the stalls by a different singer in descending order of seniority, while at the same time the nine lessons were chanted aloft in the pulpitum by a series of clerks in ascending order of seniority, the first six clothed in surplices and the last three in copes. The responsories were also nine in number, one after each lesson, alternating between two or three soloists and the choir, whose contribution was gradually truncated as each solo verse was interposed; the resulting musical structure is a type of rondo, and is particularly satisfying when, as in the first and last responsories, polyphony contrasts with plainsong. In the first responsory the verse is sung, from above the altar, by five boys bearing lighted tapers, in imitation of a choir of angels.

The Christmas of 1557 was the last that Mary would see. She died on 17 November 1558, a tragic if misguided figure, abandoned by the husband she loved, denied the child she desired, and in the knowledge that her successor would undo the religious restoration that she had laboured to achieve.

Introit *Lux fulgebit* with Gradual, Alleluia, and Offertory from the Mass at Dawn on Christmas Day. Laon Gradual, *c*. tenth century (Laon 239, f.9r)

The second Mass of Christmas (the *Missa in Aurora*) as it might have been conducted in Metz Cathedral on Saturday 25 December 902

The integrity of the Frankish Empire created by Charlemagne did not long survive his death in 814. Signs of dissolution became increasingly evident during the reign of his son and successor Louis the Pious (814–40), and in 843 the Treaty of Verdun formally recognised a partition of the imperial territories between his grandsons Lothair, Louis the German and Charles the Bold. Charles (840–77) became king of the West Franks; Louis (840–76) became king of the East Franks; and Lothair (840–55), titular emperor, became king of Italy and of a narrow strip of territory separating his brothers' kingdoms. By 875 Lothair and his own three sons were dead, and his lands north of the Alps were thereupon absorbed into the kingdoms of Charles and Louis, which grew into the medieval kingdoms of France and Germany. The imperial title survived Lothair's death, but it had little practical significance until the masterful German king Otto the Great was crowned emperor in 962 – an event that established the Holy Roman Empire of the Middle Ages and gave the kings of Germany a long-exploited justification for intervening in the affairs of the Italian peninsula.

The contribution of the Carolingian dynasty to the early medieval cultural renaissance, in particular to the standardisation of the liturgy and the expansion of the chant repertory, has already been described (see pages 24–31). One of the most influential centres in this respect was Metz, capital of the province of Lorraine, where the song-school attached to the cathedral was already being called the equal of the Roman *schola cantorum* as early as the reign of Charlemagne's father Pepin (751–68). Under Charlemagne himself, Metz played a central role in the creation and dissemination of an enlarged corpus of chant in reliable and authoritative readings. An early tenth-century noted gradual from Metz (Laon, Bibliothèque Municipale, MS 239) preserves most of the Mass Propers for the liturgical year in unusually consistent and informative notation. It enables us to place this reconstruction of the Mass at Dawn at Metz at a time when musical traditions there were still vigorous, and it allows us to attempt to recover some elements of contemporary performance practice. To appreciate this last point one needs to know something about early chant notation and modern theories regarding its interpretation. The following remarks are closely based on material by John Blackley, the editor of this reconstruction.

A fundamental problem faced the composers of liturgical chants: how to set irregularly accented prose, consisting of sacred words (not a syllable of which might be altered) to music that was often formulaic and often heavily reliant upon recurring melodic phrases. The solution, so simple that it probably evolved spontaneously, was to give to each syllable of the text a minimum rhythmic length, called a *long*, that according to context might be left as it stood, or divided into two equal *shorts*, or even augmented. Thus, if each syllable ordinarily had at least the length of a long, then the accentual pattern of the text could conform the music to itself, and the free rhythm of prose could determine the rhythm of the music.

The intentions of early copyists of chant regarding rhythm are made clear in manuscripts of the early tenth century. In these manuscripts, signs called *neumes* indicate (usually quite literally) the shapes to be traced in the air by the conductor's hand. Different note-lengths are clearly indicated in neumatic notation; that these are actually and measurably diverse lengths, rather than mere nuances, is obvious not only from the striking differences between the symbols themselves but also from the common-sense strength of the rhythmic principle outlined in the previous paragraph.

When neumatic notation was current, singers had to know the chant melodies by heart; the director's conducting served only to remind the *schola* of points of detail and movement of line. Rhythm, ornamentation and the general melodic contours can be read from these neumes, but the exact pitches and intervals of the melody cannot.

For unequivocal readings of the melodies we must turn to later but apparently congruent sources, in which less subtly expressive neumes are written with a careful regard to their relative height (diastematic notation) or on stave lines, or are accompanied by letters indicating the precise notes. Chant in these later sources may be divided into two musical dialects, distinguished by the habitual use of a minor third ('German') or a major second ('French') in certain typical musical contexts. The German dialect is likely to be the older and the closer to Carolingian tradition. The readings of our chief neumatic source, Laon 239, have therefore been compared wtith those of the very conservative, twelfth-century diastematic German dialect gradual, Graz MS 807; secondary reference has been made to the fourteenth-century Thomaskirche Graduale and the French dialect, alphabetically notated eleventh-century gradual, Montpellier MS H-159.

Although they may disagree about details of interpretation, most scholars (other than those connected with the Abbey of Solesmes) today believe that the chant written in the neumatic manuscripts was mensural; that is, it was in a free rhythm of longs and shorts, measured in some sort of proportion. The intepretation set out above is based generally upon Jan W. A. Vollaerts's *Rhythmic Proportions in Early Medieval Ecclesiastical Chant* (Leiden, 1960). While details of his theory may need correction or development, the several attempts to discredit his work have failed because they have dealt only with details and have ignored the unique capacity of proportional rhythm, as Vollaerts understood it, to declaim the texts with rhetorical accuracy and sensitivity.

Proportional-rhythm chant did, however, give way to equalist-rhythm chant (the basis of the Solesmes interpretation); the transition was probably fairly complete by the mid-eleventh century. Poor training of the choirs, the frequent relocation of monastic singers, and the ever-increasing extent of the repertory all demanded that musical memory be aided by precise pitch-notation, but as the shapes of the neumes developed, allowing pitches to be indicated more clearly, their rhythmic and ornamental significance declined. The rise of early organum – the singing of chant in parallel parts – not only served as a distraction from the subtle art of proportional rhythm, but also effectively encouraged an equalization of rhythmic values. Equalist rhythm chant is, simply, a later tradition of chant singing; though certainly legitimate, it seems not to reflect the practice expressed in the earliest extant manuscripts.

In this reconstruction of the Mass at Dawn the items of the Proper have been taken, as described above, from Laon MS 239; the Ordinary chants have been chosen for their simplicity and comparative antiquity. Texts for the prayers and Preface are taken from the ninth-century Drogo Sacramentary, and the structure of the service is based on the eighth-century Metz Sacramentary. The Reverend Thomas J. Talley, of the General Theological Seminary in New York City, graciously consented to act as liturgical consultant.

Part of medieval Rheims, showing the cathedral (right of centre) with the cloisters on the north side (east is at the top of the page). *Theatrum exhibens celebriores Galliae et Helvetiae*, Amsterdam, 1650 (British Library, C25.b12)

The Procession and Third Mass of Christmas, as they might have been conducted in Rheims Cathedral on Saturday 25 December 1361

The principal town of the county of Champagne, medieval Rheims was the thriving centre of a prosperous region whose fairs attracted merchants and travellers from all Europe and beyond. In the twelfth and thirteenth centuries the counts of Champagne had been powerful and sometimes disruptive influences in the French kingdom, but through the marriage between Joan of Navarre, heiress to Champagne, and the future King Philip IV in 1284, the county had become a royal possession. Rheims was more than a busy commercial town; it was an ecclesiastical centre of great antiquity and prestige, in whose cathedral and by whose archbishops the kings of France were traditionally crowned (a custom stemming from the baptism at Rheims of Clovis, first of the Merovingian kings of France, by Archbishop Remigius in 496). The magnificent gothic cathedral dedicated to Our Lady, begun in 1211, was still being embellished in the fourteenth century; it was considered the chief glory of the town, perhaps rather unfairly overshadowing the more old-fashioned splendours of the abbey church of St Remi. Like most other urban centres, Rheims suffered greatly during the Black Death (1348–51), but it soon returned to something like its former prosperity, particularly during the lull in Anglo-French hostilities that began with the signing of the Treaty of Bretigny in 1360.

Guillaume de Machaut's association with Rheims appears to have been life-long. In all probability he was born there or nearby in about 1300, and it was at Rheims that he died in 1377. It may well have been at the cathedral that he received the education and professional training that led to his appointment as a secretary to John, Duke of Luxembourg and King of Bohemia, in about 1323. As a member of John's household he quickly gained a reputation as a poet, composer, and musician, and it is likely that the more mundane of his secretarial duties diminished as his artistic reputation increased. King John obviously valued him highly, procuring for him several benefices, including a canonry in Rheims Cathedral, in which he was installed in 1337. In about 1340 Machaut took up residence in Rheims and ceased to be a full-time member of John's household, although he continued to serve the King until the latter's heroic death at the Battle of Crécy in 1346. Thereafter Machaut had several patrons, including John's daughter Bonne; King Charles the Bad of Navarre; John, Duke of Berry; Amadeus VI, Count of Savoy; and the future King Charles V of France. The last of these even visited Machaut's house in Rheims in 1361, the year in which our reconstruction is set. Little is known of Machaut's relations with these patrons; he probably spent most of his time at home, supplying

45

literary and musical works on request, and visiting their courts more as an honoured guest than as a paid servant.

His lengthy period of residence in Rheims shows that Machaut was far from being an absentee canon, and there is no reason to suspect that he was an inactive member of the chapter. He and his brother Jean (who had also been in the employ of John of Luxembourg) gave money for the building of the Lady Chapel of the cathedral, and his *Messe de Nostre Dame* is most likely to have been written for performance there. Nothing is known about the circumstances in which the Mass was written; there is no evidence to support the old claim that it was composed for the coronation of Charles V in 1364. There is, in fact, no proof that Machaut wrote the entire Mass at one particular time, or that he always intended the six movements to go together. The movements do not constitute a cyclic Mass of the Renaissance type, for they have neither thematic interrelation nor consistency of style or technique. The work is perhaps most realistically seen as an assembly of individual movements brought together for a specific purpose, like other fourteenth-century masses such as the *Mass of Tournai* and the *Mass of Barcelona*. The title of the Mass has commonly (and probably quite correctly) been taken to imply that Machaut meant the work primarily to be sung on one of the feasts of Our Lady. At Rheims several of these feasts, including the Assumption, the Annunciation, and the Nativity, were given the highest possible grading, providing for especially elaborate ceremonial including the singing of the *Laudes regiae*; and on such occasions it would have been considered appropriate further to enhance the ceremony by singing polyphonic music. Several other feasts, however, including Easter Day and Christmas Day, also received this supreme grading, and these would also have been regarded as suitable occasions for polyphony. Since there is no evidence to suggest that Machaut's setting was used exclusively as a Marian Mass, we have no compunction in using it to heighten the festive mood of the third Mass of Christmas.

In this reconstruction the Proper plainchant for the Mass comes from a fourteenth-century Rheims gradual (Rheims, Bibliothèque Municipale, MS 224), but the extremely corrupt version of the Sequence given in this manuscript has been amended with reference to a mid-thirteenth-century proser from the Sainte Chappelle, now in the Chapter Library at Bari. The *Laudes regiae* have been taken from a Rheims proser of the fourteenth century (Assisi, Biblioteca Comunale, MS 695). The order of service follows the Rheims customary, but (in the absence of a Rheims source) the chants themselves have been taken from an English processional (Oxford, Bodleian Library, MS Bodley 637). Machaut's setting of the Ordinary is, as he must have intended, sung by a small group of unaccompanied voices.

The Procession and Mass of St Stephen, as they might have been conducted in the Chapel of St Stephen in the Palace of Westminster on Sunday 26 December 1529

The Palace of Westminster was a royal residence from the time of its building by Edward the Confessor until the reign of Henry VIII. In 1529 Henry stole York House from Cardinal Wolsey, renamed it Whitehall Palace and lived there instead. Like every royal palace, Westminster had a chapel in which the devotions of the household were performed, and a permanent chapel staff to conduct them. The chapel at Westminster was founded by King Stephen and dedicated to St Stephen. Its reconstruction on a grand scale began in 1292 under Edward I and was completed in 1347 by his grandson Edward III, who in 1348 created a college (or community) of a dean and twelve canons, thirteen vicars, four clerks and six choristers to carry out the services with appropriately regal dignity.

When the college was dissolved in 1547, Edward VI gave St Stephen's Chapel to the Commons for their meetings (previously they had used the chapter house of Westminster Abbey), and they continued to meet there until 1834, when the entire palace – except for Westminster Hall and the crypt and cloisters of the chapel – was burnt down. The Houses of Parliament were built on the site of the old palace, with the present St Stephen's Hall (along which visitors pass on their way to the Central Lobby) precisely where the chapel had been. The lofty vaulting of the hall and its imposing length (95 feet) give some idea of what the chapel itself must have been like. The little chapel in the crypt below is still used for the marriages of MPs and the christenings of their children. To the north lie the magnificent fan-vaulted cloisters, completed in 1529 after three years' work, around which (in this reconstruction) the procession will pass.

It is probable that – as in most royal chapels – the choir of St Stephen's increased in number during the fifteenth and early sixteenth centuries to keep abreast of musical fashion, in particular with the evolution of a highly ornate style of sacred polyphony in five, six, or even more parts (a style best known today from the music of John Taverner, c.1495–1545). An interesting aspect of developments at St Stephen's is that during the fifteenth century the post of virger seems to have become a specifically musical appointment, perhaps in order to obtain the services of a skilled musician and choirmaster without having to amend the college statutes (which had been written before such a need existed). The composer John Bedyngham had been virger in the 1460s, and Nicholas Ludford was named as virger in the dissolution list of 1547.

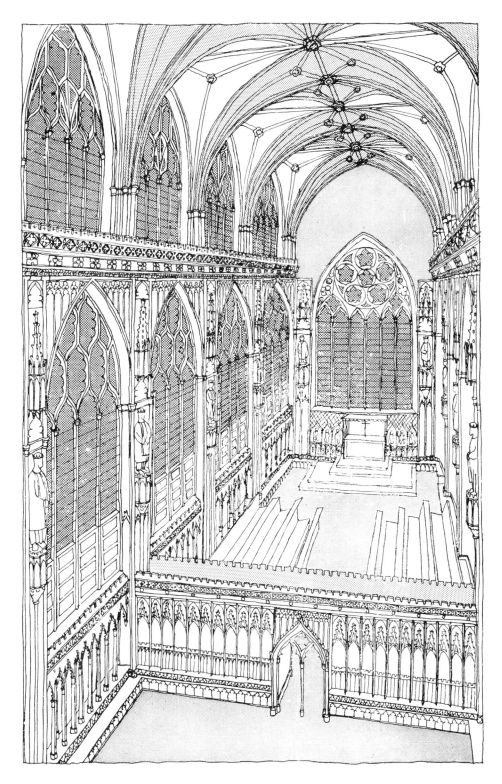

Nowadays Ludford is a forgotten figure, but he was one of the finest composers of Taverner's generation. Very little is known of Ludford's career, but the chances are that he worked at St Stephen's for a large part of it; the Mass *Lapidaverunt Stephanum*, which is very unlikely to have been written for any other institution, occurs in a manuscript copied not much later than 1520. It is this Mass that we hear in the reconstruction. Like most English masses of the period, it is based on a plain-song cantus firmus, one of the antiphons from Lauds on St Stephen's Day. For most of the time this is given to the tenor part, but it rises once to the top of the texture and is heard very clearly in the treble part in equal note-values; this happens in the Sanctus, at the words 'Benedictus qui venit in nomine Domini', and it may be that Ludford was alluding to the fact that these are the closing words of the day's Gospel reading. Ludford sets the Gloria, Credo, Sanctus, and Agnus Dei, the troped Kyrie being left in plainsong. The music is sonorous and ornate, with a great deal of contrast between five-part tutti sections and passages for two and three voices. Ludford may not quite match Taverner in the logic and cogency of his melodic writing, but there is real warmth and individuality in his harmonic style. Like all royal chapels, St Stephen's followed Salisbury use, as we have in this reconstruction.

Conjectural drawing by Ian Hodgson of St Stephen's Chapel, Westminster *c.* 1348–1547. Maurice Hastings, *Parliament House* (Architectural Press, 1950)

The Mass of St John the Evangelist, as it might have been conducted at Innsbruck by the Holy Roman Emperor Maximilian I on Thursday 27 December 1509

The Holy Roman Empire was created on Christmas Day 800, when Pope Leo III rewarded Charlemagne, king of the Franks, for his help against the Lombards by crowning him Emperor of the West and hailing him 'Caesar Augustus'. This recreation of the old Western Empire was in name only; Charlemagne's domain had its centre in eastern France, not in Italy, and (having no underlying administrative, racial, linguistic, or cultural unity) it simply fell apart after his death. But the title was potent in its implication of a temporal overlordship in Europe to complement the spiritual leadership of the papacy. In 962 it was revived for the benefit of Otto, king of Germany (who like Charlemagne had been invited to pacify Italy), and thereafter it remained a constant force in European politics throughout the Middle Ages and Renaissance. Essentially the imperial dignity was an added distinction conferred upon the kings of Germany; whether the emperor could convert its political potential into reality depended upon his own strength in relation to that of other rulers, above all to that of the papacy. For what had begun as an alliance soon turned into a continuing rivalry, as emperors and popes competed for the control of Italy, drawing other powers into the struggle as alliances were made and broken. By the fifteenth century the title had become practically hereditary in the Habsburg family, the dominant landowners in Austria, because their resources enabled them better than their rivals to maintain the prestige of the office.

Nevertheless, during the long reign (1440-93) of Maximilian's father Friedrich III, the power and prestige of the emperor were at rock bottom. The division of the Hapsburg patrimony among several heirs in the fourteenth century left him short of money and influence. Defied by his nominal subjects, threatened by a resurgent France and an ambitious Burgundy, the penniless emperor could not even afford to keep a state concomitant with his dignity. When he met his bride-to-be on the way to his coronation at Rome in 1452, her entourage was humiliatingly larger than his own. His court retinue, including his chapel and musical establishment, may well have been smaller than those of several of his vassals, such as Duke Sigmund of Tyrol and the counts of Savoy. The young Maximilian, born in 1459, must have found his upbringing in such circumstances profoundly unsettling, and this probably explains some of the peculiarities of his character in later years.

Maximilian seems to have been something of an enigma both to his contemporaries and to later historians. He is reputed not to have spoken until his tenth year, yet later he became a competent linguist; he gloried in the ostentation of the imperial dignity, but he was always short of money; he conceived bold projects but lacked the means and the resolution to carry them through (as in 1508, when his planned journey to Rome for his coronation foundered on the Venetians' refusal to let him pass through their territory). His diplomacy could be brilliant (as when he outwitted Henry VIII in 1516–17), or ineffectual (as in his expensive and unproductive involvement in the League of Cambrai). As capable of cynical realism as any Renaissance prince, he could nevertheless invent and pursue designs of astounding impracticality, such as his attempt to become pope on the death of Julius II. In his later years he seems to have retreated more and more into a fantasy world. The *Weißkunig*, a biography of him completed in about 1514 with his active participation and encouragement, already mingles fiction and fact; but the semi-autobiographical *Teuerdank* of 1517 elaborates some of his early adventures into a fantastic tale of medieval knight-errantry. Maximilian's achievements were however, solid enough. By a combination of marriage, purchase, and conquest he consolidated and extended the Habsburg possessions and made the imperial authority again a reality rather than a theoretical concept. He outlived his main rivals, Louis XII of France and Pope Julius II, and when he himself died in 1519 he bequeathed to his son Charles V a domain more extensive than it had been since the days of Charlemagne.

Like any ambitious ruler of the period, Maximilian maintained a lavish household to enhance his prestige. He probably began building up his own chapel and musical establishment after 1486, when he was elected King of the Romans (a title habitually bestowed upon the recognised heir to the imperial crown). His lengthy stay at the Burgundian court following his marriage to the young duchess, Mary, in 1477, must have opened his eyes to the ways in which music and religious ceremonial could be employed to heighten the mystique of aristocratic rule. When in 1490 he bought the Tyrol from Archduke Sigmund he seems to have taken over at least a part of Sigmund's sizeable musical staff, including the court organist and composer Paul Hofhaimer. With the death of his father in 1493 Maximilian became *de facto* Emperor, and he probably took into his service the best of whatever musicians Friedrich had possessed. During the 1490s Maximilian was constantly adding to his household to make it worthy of an emperor. In 1494 the renowned composer Heinrich Isaac joined the chapel; he continued to be associated with it until his death in 1517, although he was not always in residence. The young Ludwig Senfl became a treble in the chapel in about 1496; he remained with Maximilian throughout the latter's life and was the most eminent of the resident composers.

In 1498 the Emperor took an important step by stationing the imperial chapel (Hofkapelle) permanently in the imperial palace (Hofburg) in Vienna, and by providing it with a song-school for training and educating its choristers. This was part of a scheme initiated by Friedrich III for making Vienna the capital of the Empire (previously the town had not been of outstanding importance, and until 1513 it was

Imperator Cæsar Diuus Maximlianus, pius, fœlix, Auguſtus Chriſtianitatis ſupremus, Princeps Germanie
Hungarie, Dalmatie, Croacie, &c. Princeps potentiſſimus, tranſijt, Anno Chriſti Domini M.D.XIX. Die xij
Menſis Ianuarij, Regni Romani. XXXIII. Hungarie vero XXIX. Vixit Annis LIX. Menſibus ix, Diebus xix

not even a bishopric). Despite these moves, Maximilian himself seems not to have liked Vienna very much; he preferred Augsburg, Linz, and above all, Innsbruck, the capital of his beloved Tyrol. Although the Hofkapelle was based at Vienna, it moved around to join the Emperor on important occasions wherever he happened to be.

Maximilian spent Christmas 1509 at Innsbruck, and in this reconstruction we have assumed that the Hofkapelle joined him. At this period the chapel probably had from twelve to fifteen singers, about half of whom were boys. The organ seems to have been used in services, both in alternation with the singers and in conjunction with them. Until well into the sixteenth century the imperial chapel observed the use of Passau; our versions of the plainchant and the texts follow the Passau Gradual of 1511 and the Passau Missal of 1503. The Introit and Communion are sung to settings by Ludwig Senfl, while the Kyrie, Gloria, Sanctus, and Agnus Dei are sung to a *Missa de Apostolis* by Heinrich Isaac.

Emperor Maximilian I attending Mass in the Imperial Chapel. Paul Hofhaimer is seated at the regal, and the choir stands around a lectern. Engraving from the *Weißkunig*, c. 1514 (British Museum, 1902.4.1.6)

West front of Mexico City Cathedral, built 1573–1790 (nineteenth-century photograph)

The Aspersion and the Mass of the Holy Innocents, as they might have been conducted in Mexico City Cathedral on Sunday 28 December 1656

The Spanish conquest of the Aztec kingdom of Mexico was carried out between 1519 and 1521. Hernando Cortes, the leader of the invaders, had brought priests and musicians with him, and from the outset the Christian liturgy was celebrated according to the use of Seville. Spanish musical and liturgical customs were rapidly introduced and disseminated. Native inhabitants were soon accepted as instrumentalists and music-copyists, but at first most of the singers were Spanish-trained clergy. The first music school in the New World was established in Mexico City by Pedro de Gante, a member of the household chapel of the Emperor Charles V, in 1523; a printing press was set up there in 1539; and the first plainsong book was published in 1556. In Hernando Franco (1523–86), *maestro* of Mexico City Cathedral from 1576 until his death, the New World had its first composer of major stature.

The setting of the Ordinary to be heard in this reconstruction is by one of Franco's successors, Franciso López y Capillas. López was born in 1612, and it is now known that he was Mexican by birth; he was, in fact, the first major composer produced by the New World itself. He was already a priest by the time of his first recorded appointment (in December 1641) as organist and *bajonista* (bassoonist) in the choir of Puebla Cathedral under Juan Gutierrez de Padilla, *maestro* from 1629 to 1644 and himself a fine composer. In 1648 López left Puebla for Mexico City, and in April 1654 he himself became *maestro* of the cathedral there – a post he held until his death in about 1674.

López's surviving works include eight masses, eight Magnificats, a number of motets and hymns, and a set of choruses for the Passion according to St Matthew. Unlike Padilla, López seems to have avoided homophonic double-choir music in the Baroque manner of Italy and early seventeenth-century Spain, preferring instead to develop the polyphonic style of late sixteenth-century composers such as Palestrina. Not only are two of his masses based on motets by Palestrina – *Benedicta sit sancta Trinitas* and *Quam pulchri sunt* – but López occasionally indulges in demonstrations of technique, such as canonic writing and the use of old-fashioned notational devices. Although he sometimes writes in a more modern harmonic language, his style is essentially extremely conservative. His most complex and traditional composition is his 'Mass upon the Hexachord', *Super scalam Aretinam*, a work which he defended and explained in a learned 'declaration' copied into a Mexico City Cathedral choirbook (Choirbook VII). His most modern work is the

Missa Batalla, which is written in a rapid declamatory style typical of Spanish early Baroque music.

Although most of López's music survives in choirbooks in Mexico, the prime source of his masses and Magnificats is a beautifully written choirbook that was sent to Spain in his lifetime and is now kept in the National Library at Madrid. It is a large manuscript, a presentation copy sent in support of an application from López to the King for a full cathedral prebend; the application was granted just before the composer's death. The manuscript was prepared by three scribes, and there are many beautiful engravings of exquisite penmanship in the ornate initial letters and miniature illustrations. Native Mexican influence is reflected in the fanciful representations of animals and birds, including 'lions', frogs, turtles, serpents and even a whale. All the music, however, is in the conservative manner that persisted in the Spanish Empire, and it contains no hints of native influence or material.

López's Mass *Alleluia*, to be heard in this reconstruction, is for five voices with divided trebles (*tiples*). It is based on a short Alleluia by López himself, not on his villancico-style motet *Alleluia: Dic nobis Maria*. It is written in a smoothly flowing, polyphonic style using an almost obsessive rising motif of rapid notes; by European standards of the time it is a thoroughly old-fashioned piece. It would be quite wrong to claim for it any real originality, but it is exuberant and typical of church music in the far-flung Spanish dominions.

At the sprinkling of holy water before Mass the antiphon *Asperges me* is sung in a setting by the Portuguese composer Duarte Lobo (*c.* 1563–1646), choirmaster at Lisbon Cathdral from 1594, whose fame enabled him to have handsome editions of his music published in the Spanish Netherlands by Plantin of Antwerp (Portugal was, of course, part of the Spanish Empire between 1580 and 1640). Lobo's music was widely known in Mexico, Guatemala and Peru in the seventeenth century, and it is represented in many Mexican manuscripts of the period. This setting was first printed in his second collection of masses, published in 1639.

The music to be performed at the Elevation, between the Sanctus and Benedictus, is from a choirbook in Puebla Cathedral (*Libro de Coro III*), but is actually by Hernando Franco. It consists of verses from the Office of the Dead, here performed by instruments alone as a memorial for the Innocents at the solemn moment of the Elevation of the Host. The instrumental performance of vocal music was widely practised in the Spanish dominions at least from the period when Francisco Guerrero was choirmaster at Sevill (1574-99), if not earlier.

The versions of the chant and the recitation tones used in this reconstruction are based upon those given in Spanish and Mexican manuscript choirbooks of the period, and in particular upon those in the *Graduale Dominicale* edited by Juan Hernandez in accordance with the Tridentine regulations and printed by Pedro Ocharte in 1576. In this edition the music appears in square notation, not always well registered, upon five-line staves. The chant melodies are not radically different from those in the modern *Liber Usualis*, but there is some variance and some truncation of melisma, and the text underlay often diverges in points of detail.

In the well-documented Hispanic manner, the polyphonic music is performed with voices doubled by a variety of wind instruments. The organ, the bassoon, and frequently the harp provided standard accompaniment in Spanish, Portuguese and New World cathedrals. There is also considerable evidence that the organ accompanied plainsong. Coimbra University possesses a manuscript which shows that plainsong was accompanied with an unfigured *basso seguente* in square notation, and that the chant itself was sometimes inflected with sharps and flats. Our reconstruction of this practice has necessarily to be partly conjectural, but recent research has made it possible to do this with some confidence.

The editor wishes to acknowledge the help of Jo Ann Smith of Los Angeles (who provided the transcriptions of López's music) and Professor Robert Snow (who advised on the plainchant sources), and the kindness of Don Roberto Rivera y Rivera.

The Procession and Mass of St Thomas of Canterbury, as they might have been conducted in Canterbury Cathedral on Sunday 29 December 1420

A major gap in our knowledge of medieval English liturgy is that we know almost nothing of the customs and plainchant of Canterbury Cathedral, mother-church of England and seat of its primate. The Protestant 'reformers' and the Puritans did their work too well: for the late medieval period we have no documents describing the cathedral's rite or ceremonial, and (apart from a twelfth-century gradual now at Durham) no Canterbury chant-book survives in anything like a complete state. To attempt a 'reconstruction' in these circumstances is ambitious, if not foolhardy!

Canterbury was one of the nine cathedrals of medieval England that were also Benedictine monasteries, the bishop being titular abbot but contenting himself with administering the diocese while the prior ran the cathedral and its monastic community. This system could work perfectly well, especially if (as was often the case with archbishops of Canterbury) the incumbent of the see was a royal servant, often absent on government business. Henry Chichele, archbishop from 1414 until his death in 1443, spent more time in his diocese than many medieval bishops did, and he was a generous benefactor to his cathedral, but he was also a close and trusted associate of Henry V, and led several important missions to France and Rome. A number of Chichele's predecessors had found it difficult if not impossible to serve the interests of both church and state, and in at least one case the conflict of loyalties proved fatal. As Chancellor of England between 1155 and 1162, Thomas Becket had been a faithful and diligent servant of the Crown, but when Henry II made him Archbishop of Canterbury (in order to bring the church under royal control), Thomas transferred his allegiance wholeheartedly to the church and resigned the chancellorship, the better to defend the autonomy of the church against the encroachments of the King. Relations between Henry and Thomas grew so bad that in 1165 the latter went into self-imposed exile in France. In 1170 a reconciliation was arranged, and the Archbishop returned to England early in December. Resentment was quickly rekindled on both sides, however, and on Tuesday 29 December 1170, Thomas was murdered in his own cathedral by four of the King's knights. This sacrilege shocked and revolted Europe; within three years Thomas had been canonised and miracles at his tomb had begun to be reported. In 1174 Henry himself, probably motivated as much by love for the man who had been his companion as by political necessity, came to do public penance before the relics of the saint.

Thomas's reputation as a pious defender of the church and champion of the poor made his cult enormously popular. His tomb became one of the major centres of

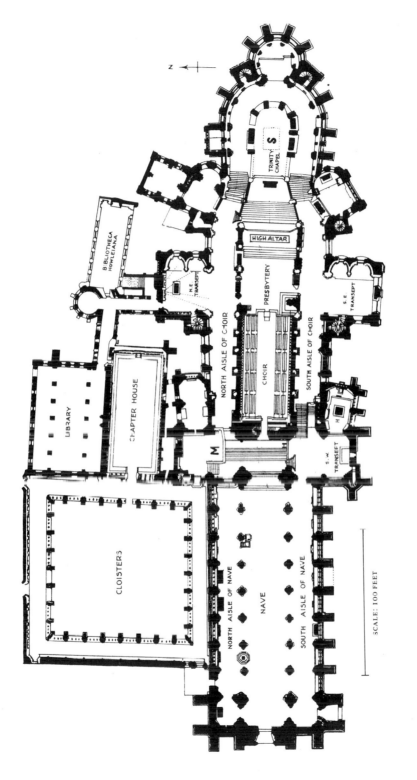

Plan of Canterbury Cathedral (after W. D. Caröe, 1925). The site of Becket's martyrdom is marked 'M'; the site of the shrine is marked 'S'.

pilgrimage in England and an unparalleled source of revenue for the monastery. Fifty years after the martyrdom the bones were transferred with great ceremony to a splendid shrine in the Trinity Chapel, to the east of the high altar, in the presence of the young King Henry III; here they remained until the agents of another Henry despoiled the shrine and scattered the relics in 1538. The translation of the relics on 7 July 1220 became known as the first jubilee of St Thomas, and subsequent jubilees were held every fifty years until 1470, that of 1420 being the fifth. Although the jubilee celebrations took place on the feast of the translation rather than on that of the martyrdom, it seems likely that in a jubilee year the latter anniversary would also have been commemorated with special ceremony. (For an account of these occasions, see Raymonde Foreville, *Le Jubilé de Saint Thomas Becket*, Paris, 1958.)

The cathedral's importance was enhanced by Canterbury's position on the main road between London and Dover, the usual port for travellers to and from northern France. Aristocratic travellers, including princes and monarchs, often spent their first or last night in England at Canterbury, usually in the guest-house of the cathedral or in the bishop's palace, or at the neighbouring abbey of St Augustine. In 1420 (the year of our reconstruction) many of those present would have remembered the visit four years earlier of King Henry V and the Holy Roman Emperor Sigismund, and the signing of a treaty between them. Many members of the nobility came not merely as passing travellers but as pilgrims, to make their devotions and offerings at the shrine as ordinary people did, and as Henry VIII was to do in 1520.

Our lack of information about the cathedral's liturgy in the later Middle Ages is particularly ironic, because we know more about its musical life than we do about that of most other institutions of the period. Some of our knowledge comes from musical fragments and administrative documents in the cathedral archives, but one of the most interesting sources is a chronicle kept between 1415 and 1471 by John Stone, one of the monks of the community. Stone was unusually interested in music (he may conceivably have been the composer of this name whose music appears in two Continental manuscripts), and he has much to say about musical affairs in the monastery. From him, for example, we learn that John Boorne, who died in September 1420 after being precentor for some thirty years, had no training in polyphony but was a fine singer, whereas his successor John Stanys (who died in December 1421) was skilled in part-music and made the cathedral famous for its polyphony. Stone names other practitioners of polyphony and even gives the titles and composers of pieces sung on certain occasions. He also records the death in 1445 of Lionel Power, one of the most famous composers associated with the cathedral. Power seems to have been in charge of a special Lady Chapel choir there in the late 1430s, and he had certainly had connections with the cathedral since the early 1420s, although the precise nature of these is uncertain. The settings by Power of the Gloria, Credo, Sanctus, and Agnus Dei sung in this reconstruction come from the Old Hall Manuscript, a collection of Mass music probably compiled for the household chapel of Thomas, Duke of Clarence, between about 1415 and 1420. As the second son of Henry IV and heir-presumptive to Henry V, Thomas was a major figure in the politics of his time, until his death in battle against the French in 1421 removed him from the scene. Power was a member of his chapel at about the time when the Old Hall Manuscript was being copied. There is no evidence that this music was ever sung at Canterbury, but in view of Power's link with the cathedral and Clarence's frequent visits there, as well as the fact that the Gloria and Credo employ chants from the Office of St Thomas as cantus firmi, the possibility is attractive. The anonymous motet *Post missarum* (a substitute for the usual response that ends the Mass) comes from the same manuscript.

To assemble a picture of what may have happened at Canterbury on such an occasion, we must use evidence from other institutions and from earlier in the cathedral's own history. Although Benedictine monasteries did not share a standardised liturgy, there were many similarities between their customs, and we can gain some impression of the conduct of a major feast by referring to surviving books from other Benedictine cathedrals like Worcester, Norwich, and Durham, and the larger abbeys such as St Albans, St Peter's at Gloucester, and St Mary's at York. Valuable information about earlier practice at Canterbury itself is given in the constitutions drawn up by Lanfranc during his archiepiscopate (1070–89). However, Lanfranc was concerned less with pure liturgy than with the general life of the community; and, of course, he has nothing to say about St Thomas.

In this reconstruction we have pieced together from several sources a procession and Mass for St Thomas that is generally Benedictine rather than specifically Canterburian. In no sense is it authentic or definitive; it merely tries to give an idea of what such a celebration may have been like. The items of the Proper come from a manuscript from St Peter's, Gloucester (Oxford, Bodleian Library, MS Jesus College 10). The tones for the Preface, *Pater noster*, and *Pax* are from a manual from St Augustine's, Canterbury (Bodleian Library, MS Barlow 32). The order for the procession has been conflated from Lanfranc's *Constitutions*, and the Ordinal of St Mary's Abbey, York (Cambridge, St John's College, MS D.27); and the processional chants are from an early fifteenth-century Salisbury processional (London, British Library, MS Add. 57534). We may perhaps imagine the Mass being celebrated by Prior John Woodnesbergh (1411–28), since Archbishop Chichele seems to have spent Christmas 1420 at his palace at Otford.

Responsory *Protector noster*, for Mass on the Sunday after Christmas. Ambrosian gradual, fourteenth century (Bodleian Library, MS Lat. Lit. c.34, f.35r)

The Mass on the Sunday after Christmas, as it might have been conducted in the Winter Church at Milan on Sunday 30 December 1128

Milan was one of the very few ecclesiastical centres to preserve virtually intact its ancient liturgy and chant throughout the Middle Ages. To maintain independence was, in fact, as much of a priority for the spiritual leaders of the city as it was for its temporal lords; bishops in the Dark Ages resisted the Lombards no less fiercely than the Visconti and Sforza dukes of later centuries resisted the encroachments of the papacy and neighbouring territories. From the time of St Ambrose, a successful and popular provincial governor who occupied the see from 374 until his death in 397, the archbishops of Milan played a crucial role in the city's history. In the eighth century they led the opposition to the Lombards and to the Arian heresy that the invaders espoused. When Charlemagne came to Italy to crush the Lombards it was Archbishop Eugenius who managed to persuade him not to suppress the Milanese rite in favour of that of Rome. In the tenth century Eugenius's successors were prominent in the coalition of north Italian bishops which, at a time when the reputation and influence of the papacy were at a very low ebb, took the initiative in trying to bring peace to the region. This involved asking the German king Otto the Great to come and restore order (in 951), a fateful step that was to result in 963 in the conferring on him of the imperial title. It was another Milanese archbishop, Aribert, who in 1025 invited another emperor, Conrad II, to Italy to be invested with the Iron Crown of Lombardy. In 1277 Archbishop Ottone Visconti led the nobles to victory over the republican party and made his family masters of the city for the next 170 years.

St Ambrose himself had been a vehement opponent of Arianism and a fearless critic of injustice and corruption. On one famous occasion he refused communion to Emperor Theodosius himself. It was largely the preaching of Ambrose that converted St Augustine of Hippo to Christianity. In the Middle Ages the prestige of Ambrose was such that he was credited with the creation of Milanese liturgy and its chant, which for this reason were (and still are) often called 'Ambrosian'. While this must be a major overstatement – Ambroses's extant contribution probably extends no further than the words of half a dozen hymns – a great deal of the rite is undoubtedly very ancient in origin. In addition to a basic core of locally produced material, there are chants borrowed from the eastern Church (including a few from Jerusalem itself) and from the Gallican and Mozarabic repertories between about 400 and 600. Other chants were taken over from Rome during the same period, and these have not been revived as the parent versions subsequently were at Rome. Because Ambrosian chant did not undergo the kind of revision that Roman chant experienced in the seventh century, it has many individual features which have long since been edited out of the Roman repertory; this makes it both less consistent and more prone to stylistic extremes.

In the Roman rite some categories of chant are stylistically very uniform: Communions, for example, are usually terse and simple, while Graduals are lengthy and ornate. At Milan, however, there are large variations of style within each category, from the very plain to the extremely elaborate. Ambrosian melodies are also much less susceptible to modal classification than their Roman counterparts, because they have never been modified to conform with a subsequently devised standard in the same sort of way. Where many Roman melodies have an 'average' kind of style, somewhere between syllabic and melismatic, Milanese melodies tend towards one of the two extremes, being either fairly consistently syllabic (like the Transitorium *Maria virgo* to be heard in this reconstruction), or melismatic (like the virtuoso Psalmellus *Benedictus qui venit*). The Ambrosian melodic style includes a higher proportion of stepwise motion than we find in Gregorian chant. It is also more prone to employ melodic sequence and repetition, and it prefers leaps of a fourth to the favourite Gregorian intervals of the third and the fifth. The general feeling of archaism and insularity about the rite and its music is reinforced by Milan's avoidance of troping and the Sequence, and the extreme scarcity of any polyphony until the very late Middle Ages, when it tends to take a very primitive form.

The Milanese liturgy has many individual features (the course of the Ambrosian Mass and its main constituents are described on page 27). Our main sources of information on the later medieval customs are the *Ordo* of the cathedral steward Beroldus, who was writing soon after the death of Archbishop Olricus (1120-25) and hence very close to the date of our reconstruction, and the chronicle of Landulphus senior (*c.* 1085). Beroldus is highly informative about all kinds of aspects and ramifications of the liturgy, including the step-by-step conduct of the main services and the duties of each functionary. Landulphus is usefully specific about the numbers of participants involved. Yet despite the fullness and apparent precision of these accounts, some questions are difficult to answer. In some cases the phraseology is either ambiguous or hard to believe: our performance of the Alleluia, for example, follows what we understand Beroldus to be describing, but the resulting fourfold statement of the Responsory does not tally with more recent Milanese practice; it may not be coincidence that no modern writer has discussed the performance of the Milanese Alleluia in any detail. One rather unexpected problem is that the church in which this service would have taken place has entirely disappeared. The Milanese liturgy was unique in using two churches, one in winter and the other in summer. The present Cathedral, begun in 1387 and dedicated to the Nativity of the Virgin, was built on the site of the original Winter church, the ninth-century cathedral of Santa Maria Maggiore. The fourth-century Summer church, dedicated to St Thecla, stood nearby until 1461, on what is now the Piazza del Duomo.

In our reconstruction we have assumed that like many churches of its period and locality Santa Maria Maggiore was basilican in design.

According to Beroldus, the archbishop normally officiated at the major services on Sundays and great feasts. This reconstruction, therefore, is of a Pontifical Mass. The plainchant is taken from two antiphoners: a winter half of the mid-twelfth century (London, British Library, MS Add.34209) and a summer half of the early fourteenth century (Oxford, Bodleian Library, MS Lat. Lit. c.34). In the absence of a more ancient source, the tones for the readings, prayers and versicles have been taken from the *Antiphonale Missarum ... Mediolanensis* (Rome, 1935). The tones for the Preface, *Pater noster,* Embolism, and *Pax* come from the *Missale secundum ordinem Sancti Ambrossi* (Milan, 1505), which has also been used to expand the information given by Beroldus.

Interior of the Sistine Chapel, showing the pope presiding at mass, with the singers standing in the *cantoria* on the right. Engraving by Etienne Dupérac, from Antoine Lafrèry's *Speculum Romanae magnificentiae*, 1578 (Vatican Library, Ris. Stragr. 7, f.116)

The Pontifical High Mass of St Sylvester, as it might have been conducted in the Sistine Chapel on Sunday 31 December 1615

On the last day of the old year the church honours St Sylvester (hence the German name, Sylvesterabend, for New Year's Eve). Sylvester was Pope from 314 to 335, a time when the church was first enjoying relative freedom from persecution; he was, in fact, one of the first popes not to die a martyr. In 325 he presided over the Council of Nicaea, at which the Arian heresy was finally condemned.

For this celebration of Mass we move to early seventeenth-century Rome, an appropriate setting for the feast of such a pope. The music for the Ordinary of the Mass is by Francesco Soriano, a pupil of Palestrina and one of Rome's more conservative musicians in this age of progressive styles; he directed the Cappella Giulia in St Peter's Basilica from 1603 until 1620. Soriano was noted for his use of the polyphonic style, and the eight-part Mass sung during this celebration is of particular interest because it is an arrangement, or rather a recomposition, of Palestrina's *Missa Papae Marcelli*, for double choir instead of the original six voices. It is thus an early manifestation of the esteem in which that work has so continuously been held. Soriano gives us an early Baroque view of Palestrina's Mass by transferring its material to a richer and more spacious canvas, and by adding touches of chromatic colouring. The notable feature of Palestrina's Mass, the clarity with which the text is declaimed in the Gloria and Credo, is not obscured but emphasised by Soriano's frequent use of dialogue between the two four-part choirs.

The chant for all the other musical items in the Mass has come from various Italian liturgical books, dating from the period immediately after the reforms of the Council of Trent. Despite the fact that Palestrina and Annibale Zoilo (another Roman musician) were commissioned to re-edit the standard chant books in the aftermath of the Council, no attempt was made at the time to halt the general corruption of medieval chant that had been creeping in over the centuries. Thus the melismatic items of the Proper (the Introit, Gradual, Alleluia, Offertory, and Communion) exhibit the tendencies towards drastic pruning of melisma – narrowing of vocal range, modal transposition, and alteration of word underlay to give 'correct' vocal stress – that are hallmarks of this process of corruption. This can best be appreciated in the Gradual *Ecce sacerdos*, whose original melody is the same as that of the famous Maundy Thursday Gradual *Christus factus est*; much of the elaboration of the original chant, including its remarkable soaring line, is absent. Likewise the chant for the Alleluia is brief to the point of perfunctoriness. These Proper items have been transcribed from the *Graduale Romanum* printed in Venice in 1611. Apart from a special Alleluia verse, the texts are drawn from various masses in the

Common of the Saints. This set of chants was indeed current until well into the present century, when a self-contained set beginning with the Introit *Si diligis me* was drawn up specially for the Mass of Holy Popes.

If the ornate chants are hardly recognisable from the versions found in present-day restored chant books, the remaining, routine Mass tones, including those for the chanting of the Epistle and Gospel, will be very familiar to anyone conversant with a Tridentine High Mass, for they have barely altered over the centuries. Most of them have been transcribed from the 1576 edition of the *Missale Romanum,* while the tone for the Pontifical Blessing (required at masses celebrated by a bishop or a prelate of high rank) comes from the *Pontificale* of 1595. The Gloria intonation and the melody of *Ite missa est* are assigned in the Missal to feasts of double rank, like that of St Sylvester.

The Nativity is commemorated in the second Collect, that of Christmas, which is recited daily during Christmas week, and in the Christmas Preface, which is used until the Epiphany. The Epistle, from St Paul's letter to Timothy, contains an exhortation to soundness of doctrine and ends with the famous passage, 'the time of my departure is at hand. I have fought a good fight...' The Gospel for the day is the passage from St Luke on the subject of the vigilant servant, beginning 'Let your loins be girded...'

The Mass of the Circumcision, as it might have been conducted in Beauvais Cathedral on Saturday 1 January 1228

A thirteenth-century manuscript from Beauvais Cathedral (London, British Library, MS Egerton 2615) contains the remains of a complete Office and Mass for the Feast of the Circumcision. Although it must have been copied between 1227 (it names Pope Gregory IX, who was elected in that year) and 1234 (it leaves a gap where the name of the Queen of France should be, because Louis IX did not marry until then), the manuscript clearly represents the bringing up to date of an earlier tradition and repertory stretching back at least to the mid-twelfth century. Possibly it was copied for use in the new cathedral, which was begun in 1227. Some of the pages are missing, but luckily the loss can to some extent be made good from a similar manuscript from Sens Cathedral, although this is slightly earlier (c. 1221) and less ambitious in its music. The most striking feature of the Beauvais manuscript itself is, in fact, its extraordinarily lavish provision of music for the feast, in particular the number of tropes, prosulae and additional items which it furnishes for Vespers, the post-Vespers procession, Matins and Mass. The compiler may have intended to provide an extensive stock of material, both monophonic and polyphonic, from which a selection could be made. Why was such attention paid to a day which, liturgically, was merely the octave of Christmas? At least part of the answer probably lies outside the liturgy.

For reasons which are now obscure, in the later Middle Ages and afterwards the Feast of the Circumcision was often known as the Feast of Fools, and it seems often to have been kept with great ceremony and (even in the most august of institutions) a certain light-heartedness. Some writers have seen this as a vestigial survival of the Roman Saturnalia; others have viewed it as an understandable relaxation from the joyful but solemn splendours of Christmas week itself; still others have suspected – probably with considerable justification – that some of the wilder excesses said to have been committed lay more in the wishful imagination of later commentators than in fact. The feast, in Latin *festum fatuorum*, *stultorum*, or *asinorum*, seems to have appeared first in France during the twelfth century and to have spread throughout Europe, surviving widely until the sixteenth century and in some places even until the eighteenth. The general procedure seems to have been to allow the younger clerics, particularly the subdeacons, to take over much of the conduct of the services and to permit a certain amount of levity. Special musical effects were sometimes employed: at Beauvais, for instance, the antiphons at First Vespers were sung in falsetto, a type of singing whose use in plainchant was strongly discouraged.

The Office itself was very like that of Christmas, a week earlier. The feast was often called the Office of the Baculus (the name of the precentor's baton or staff of office, which seems sometimes to have been used to beat people). It was also known as the *Deposuit*, because the Magnificat verse beginning 'Deposuit potentes' ('He has put down the mighty from their seat and exalted the humble') symbolised the takeover of power by the lower clerical orders and youths of the community. Drinking was certainly involved, as at the end of Lauds at Beauvais, when everybody stood outside the closed doors of the cathedral and four people held jugs of wine. Another feature of the feast was the entry of a wooden donkey into the church, probably ridden by the Lord of the Feast and certainly accompanied at Beauvais by the famous conductus *Orientis partibus*. This may have been an old tradition imported from Byzantium, for we hear of a captain of the guard in Constantinople in the ninth century being chosen as a mock patriarch and riding through the city on a white ass. Could this have been connected with the title *festum asinorum*?

Whatever elements were imported into the feast from the world outside, it was clearly in performance a sacred Office, indeed a very full one, containing numerous tropes, prosulae, conductus and motets and other polyphonic pieces. The connection of the reforming archbishop Pierre de Corbeil with the Sens version suggests that there at least the profane elements would have been minimised. It seems likely that at Beauvais Bishop Milo, a trusted associate of Louis VIII and a zealous supporter of the rights and prestige of his church (he died on the way to Rome to complain about royal infringement of the rights of the chapter), would also have wished dignity to prevail.

In this reconstruction items which are missing from the Beauvais manuscript have been supplied from other sources. The Introit *Puer natus est* was used on this day at Sens, as was *Kyrie Cunctipotens* at Bayeux (in the absence of a Beauvais order, the description of the procession also follows Bayeux). In a few cases Beauvais gives a monophonic setting of a particular item, but its rubrics allow for polyphonic performance; in these instances polyphonic settings of these texts have been taken from other, roughly contemporary, manuscripts. The two-part *Kyrie Cunctipotens* is in the Codex Calixtinus; the two-part Gradual trope *Viderunt Emanuel* is from the St Martial manuscript, Paris, Bibliothèque Nationale, MS lat. 3549; and the three-part Alleluia *Dies sanctificatus* occurs in several of the Notre Dame sources. This kind of substitution is exactly the same as that which the Beauvais scribe must have envisaged when he copied extra polyphonic settings of texts which he already possessed in monophonic versions. In *Haec est virga* the lower of the two voices has been added editorially to create the kind of polyphony that singers of the period sometimes improvised.

Manuscript illumination of the Circumcision. Flemish Book of Hours of the Virgin Mary, fourteenth century (British Library, MS Add. 19416, f.65r)

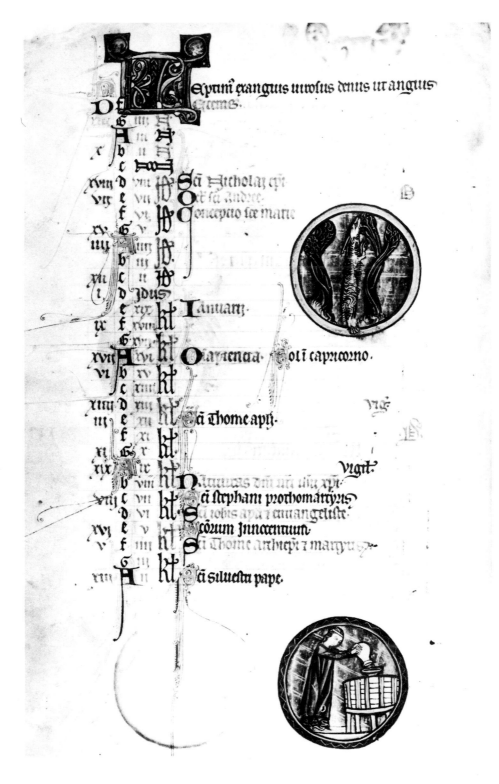

KL eptimi exanguis uirosus denus ut anguis
Cremo.

Sci Nicholai epi
et sci Andree.
Conceptio see marie

Ianuarii

Sapientia Sol i capricorno.

ā Thome apti.

Natiuitas dni ūri ihu xpi
ā stephani prothomartyris
ā Iohis apti et euangeliste
scōrum Innocentum
ā Thome archepi et martyris

ā siluestri pape.